T0193947

Get CONSCIOUS

*Wake up to your Personal Power,
Magnificence and Divine Connection*

2nd Edition

Dr. Risha Joshi

BALBOA
PRESS

A DIVISION OF HAY HOUSE

Balboa Press books may be ordered through booksellers or by contacting:

Balboa Press
A Division of Hay House
1663 Liberty Drive
Bloomington, IN 47403
www.balboapress.com
1 (877) 407-4847

Because of the dynamic nature of the Internet, any web addresses or links contained in this book may have changed since publication and may no longer be valid. The views expressed in this work are solely those of the author and do not necessarily reflect the views of the publisher, and the publisher hereby disclaims any responsibility for them.

The author of this book does not dispense medical advice or prescribe the use of any technique as a form of treatment for physical, emotional, or medical problems without the advice of a physician, either directly or indirectly. The intent of the author is only to offer information of a general nature to help you in your quest for emotional and spiritual well-being. In the event you use any of the information in this book for yourself, which is your constitutional right, the author and the publisher assume no responsibility for your actions.

Any people depicted in stock imagery provided by Getty Images are models, and such images are being used for illustrative purposes only.
Certain stock imagery © Getty Images.

Print information available on the last page.

ISBN: 978-1-9822-2804-0 (sc)
ISBN: 978-1-9822-2805-7 (e)

Balboa Press rev. date: 05/29/2019

Acknowledgment

This book has taken 32 years to come together. Not that I have been writing it for that long but this is the length of time that I have been on the planet. This is the length of time that I have been making and learning from my mistakes, studying and applying principles, watching and understanding the world around me, observing and querying that which has been dictated to me and experiencing life as I know it. Every single experience has landed me where I am now, where I want to be. For this I will always be grateful to ALL that life has offered, including the challenges, difficulties and discomfort.

My Father and my Mother, my Uncle and Aunt - *Bapa and Motima* - who are like my parents - have given me my foundation. Without my upbringing there is no way I would have aligned with my purpose – to help those who suffer from negative emotions, feelings of disempowerment, fear and lack of connection. To you I will always be grateful because you have taught me the value of unconditional love and have supported me in so many ways throughout my life. Thank you for having the courage to push past your anxieties, worries and fears so that I may fulfil my dreams. You gave up yours so that I could have mine. I love you and I am humbled by you. You have shown me the true meaning of strength, resilience and selflessness.

To my brother, Rishi, who I love more than life itself. You move me with your strength, love for the world and your balance. Thank you for always being there and helping me like Dad would have if he was here in the physical. I would be nothing without you.

To my parents' Guru – *Sri Ram Sharma Acharya* – thank you for showing my parents the way and for teaching them love and resilience through their difficult times. Thank you for being the light when they were in the dark.

To my Aunt, *Muni Masi* and the three jellies, *Pooj, Shiv* and *Vibz* – thank you for loving me unconditionally. You are Angels. You make me feel like I have come home.

To my Soul Tribe, *Karen Sophia, Chris, Ed, Jags, Radhika, Jag, Jannake, Alexander* and *Kenneth* who have helped me beyond belief. You have made me stronger and given me the confidence to carry on. You have been there to pick me up when I didn't have the strength to do it myself and you have helped me to see the way. Thank you for finding me so early on in this life. We have some amazing times ahead.

To my dog, *Winston*, you can't read this but you are adored! You mirror me back to myself and help me to evolve, like the Master you are.

To *Daisy*, you've been there for me through thick and thin. Thank you for always making me smile. I'm lucky to have you as a friend. To *Ravi*, thank you for being an oracle and always imparting your wisdom and logic without judgement. Thank you both for letting me be me and for putting up with my ways.

To *Tanay and Robert* – thank you for supporting me in all of the 'little' ways which were actually the very big ways. Thank you for listening and being a sound board. You helped me to expand my mind.

Finally, to anyone else who has loved, supported and encouraged me – I will never forget your kindness. And to anyone who has given me *any* difficult life experience - thank you for the lessons.

Above all, thank you to the Universe, for loving me throughout my life, for guiding me through my troubles and for your connection.

To all of you I dedicate this book – you are the reason why I am, where I am and for that, I will be eternally grateful.

All my love x

Contents

Dedicated to my Father,
'Lord of the Moon'

Chandresh Joshi

My Inspiration. My Source of
Strength. Always in my Heart.

Introduction

Dear Reader,

This book has been compiled with the intention to humbly assist anyone who wishes to break free from a cyclical, unfulfilling or somewhat uninspiring life. It has been written for anyone who believes that there is more to life than meets the eye and for anyone who wishes to inject passionate love into their day to day living. It is for those of you who have not yet found your purpose or your passion and are caught up in the daily grind of life without feeling much satisfaction or joy. It is for anyone who wants *more* for themselves and for others but do not feel that this is possible or that life is consistently working against you. It is for you if you feel stagnant and limited yet deeply desire to grow. This book is for you if you want to make a change but feel fearful of upsetting the 'status quo' at the risk of perceived balance and stability. It is for anyone who feels at loss in their relationships, finances, health, and levels of joy, peace or love. If this sounds like you, if you are seeking *more* from life - congratulations on taking the first step towards having a beautiful one.

I'm here to tell you that you are far more powerful and in control than you could possibly imagine. I'm here to tell you that there are no mistakes in nature – that includes yourself and your circumstances. I'm here to let you know that you are loved, supported and guided more than you could ever realise. I'm here to tell you that success is a *state of mind* and a *state of being* which is reflected in your surroundings. There is Divine order of which you are a vital component part. How can I say this with such conviction? Because there was a point in my life where I was skeptical, disconnected, depressed and felt downright hopeless. I took charge of my mind and nurtured it. Now it serves me - rather than me serving it. As a result, I feel genuine joy, excitement, love, fulfilment, peace and (most excitingly) guidance and connection *consistently* and *regularly* - and when I don't - I know how to get back to those states quickly. I took responsibility and charge of my personal suffering and decided to do something about it. The Universe met me at the level that I met myself and I have never looked back. As a result, I feel aligned with my purpose and my passion. My greatest realisation has been that in order to change my life for the better, the work was never needed outside of myself - it was *always* internal.

No matter where you are in life, it is my intention to help you realise that happiness and sadness are *choices* that we make on a day to day, minute to minute and second to second basis. The mirroring of our choices can be seen around us, in our experiences and circumstances. If you want to understand what you think about on a consistent basis - just look around you. Through the awareness of unconscious cycles of thinking that occur within the mind, it is my intention to help you realise your magnificent creative abilities and your personal power for change.

The journey from sadness to happiness, from emptiness to deep satisfaction, from fear to love, from scarcity to abundance, from despair to hope, always begin in those life changing, split-second, often 'rock bottom' moments, when we decide NO MORE. Massive change happens during these times where the pain of staying where we are is greater than the fear of change. When we reach these stages in our lives, *huge* transformation is possible. These moments in our lives are the markers of success and growth. By you acquiring this book, you have consciously or unconsciously, made a decision. You have bravely stated your intention for change. Setting off a chain reaction in the Universe.

When the mind expands, it cannot go back to its original state. By choosing to read this book, you have opened up an opportunity to expand your mind and your horizons *regardless* of whether or not the book is actually read. This desire to search is the greatest catalyst for change. I urge you to run with this opportunity, to build momentum and not to look back. It is for this reason, I thank (and encourage *you* to thank) your struggles and dissatisfaction, as without them you would not be on track to seeking the maximum fulfilment of your desires and the deep sense of satisfaction from life that is possible through continued personal expansion.

The principles outlined in this book are drawn from my own personal and also from the wisdom stored within my heart – an innate, pure wisdom that is accessible to all of us. Subsequently, the contents of the book may resonate with you at a heart and soul level. It may just feel right and make sense. If it does, I urge you to use it and continue your personal development. It is a firm belief of mine that self-investment is the best investment that any of us can make and *always* leads to success.

I have spent time, being driven by my curious mind, selecting the CORE patterns in the behaviour, mindset, teachings and mental make-up of the worlds' most successful and fulfilled people. I have presented the concepts behind their success in neat, bite-size chunks throughout this book. It is important to explain at this point, that by 'success' what I mean is our ability to accomplish any desire regardless of what is considered to be 'success' by society's standards. For some, success may mean falling in love, for others, it may mean earning a trillion dollars. No matter what you want to achieve, the concepts in this book may serve your purpose. It is my belief that the ultimate form of success is *freedom*; freedom from anything that prevents you from expanding into your greatest self. True emotional freedom leads to peace, joy, love, fulfilment and growth and these are, in my opinion, the undeniable markers of success. With these markers firmly intact *first*, any goal you put your mind to is achievable. The trick is to master the mind, which can learn to fear the '*run up*' to success and throw obstacles in the way. Undetected, the mind even has the ability to hinder it. It is in doing the necessary work at *this* level that we open ourselves up to opportunities, abundance and the fulfilment of desires – all of which are available and waiting for us in endless supply. This level of freedom is our birth right and is also the focus of this book.

Every single concept described in this book can be expanded into theses of their own but for the purpose of this book, I have attempted to make the principles easy to understand and digest, with the scope of further expansion if you wish to continue your personal inquiry. This is something that I would encourage. Just like the exponentially expanding Universe, expansion is something that we naturally desire. In its own right, it is my aim to encourage broader minded thinking and to open up your eyes to some underlying principles which, when mastered, lead to unshakeable power, deep satisfaction, increased levels of joy and abundance in all forms.

I encourage you to commit to the reading of this book and even refer back to it over time. Its digestible nature allows you to do this with ease and can act as a useful 'pick me up' during times when you feel the need to reconnect and regain perspective. Read it at a pace that feels comfortable for you and take time to absorb the concepts. This may be tricky at times as some of the ideas may tap into and even *challenge* your current belief systems which you may be relying upon, subconsciously, for emotional stability. Try to become aware of these areas of resistance and consider the prospect that the uncomfortable change is pointing you towards those aspects of yourself that warrant exploration. You may find that some of the belief systems are perfectly valid or you may find that you are unknowingly holding onto a belief that is flawed, irrelevant or outdated. *These* are the beliefs that hold you back. Give yourself time to explore your mind. The awareness of it will assist in the clearing of those mental factors that block your growth. Fundamentally, take what is useful and that which resonates with you, expand on these topics if you wish, add what is uniquely your own and discard the rest. This is true creative authenticity.

Finally, if this book serves you, please pass it on to someone else so that it may serve them too.

In the writing of this book, I am sending you buckets of love and light. I wish you a *truly* beautiful life.

In divine friendship,

Risha

Namasté

My Soul honours your soul.
I honour the place in you where the entire Universe resides.
I honour the light, love, truth, beauty and peace within you, because
it is also within me.
In sharing these things, we are united. We are the same.
We are One.

Chapter 1

Are you sleeping?

*"When everyone is thinking alike,
then no one is thinking"*

— Benjamin Franklin

Our minds are all that we have.

Everything we have done, everything we are currently doing and everything we will do, is determined by our minds. The shaping of our personalities, the depth of our interpersonal connections, the quality of our relationships, the minor and major decisions that we make and how we perceive the world, ALL depend upon our thoughts. What we think, we become. The quality of our lives is *directly* related to the quality of our thoughts.

Experience gets filtered into our minds via our senses and then interpreted, analysed and assessed. The more emotionally impactful the experience, the greater the likelihood of it becoming ingrained within our minds. Even those experiences with *zero* emotional impact get stored as is the power of the subconscious mind. These 'stored' thoughts, if called upon and repeatedly stimulated over time, become our active **beliefs** about the various aspects of life that we have had exposure to. They become our convictions and our versions of 'truth'. These experiences and their interpretations, become the models for our lives and influence our view of the world as a whole. The way in which we process our experiences i.e. *how* we view our personal stories and the meanings that we attach to them, play a huge role in our outlook and the lens through which we experience life. Depending on the nature of our beliefs, they either help us to grow and expand or they restrict and contract us.

Over time, we have become highly efficient accumulators of experience, thoughts, feelings and beliefs. We use our experiences and our interpretations of them to guide our lives and to form our identities. Although of referential benefit, it may be clear to see that these added 'layers' have the ability to conceal our raw, authentic nature. It may also be clear to see that if we place too much importance on our 'mental accumulation' we risk suppressing our ability to grow beyond them. Over time, we learn how to act, look, think and behave based on what we have adopted from our childhood, our historic experience and our external environment. Our ability to detach from those thoughts that limit us is *directly* related to our capacity to feel happiness, joy, peace, love and our capacity to grow – growth being the marker of all forms of success. When we can observe and consciously sort through the contents of our mind, we can become powerful orchestrators of our lives via the selection of *high quality* thoughts that encourage our expansion. By raising our awareness to include the mind, we exercise the power of choice.

When we are unaware of our minds, our interpretations of experience can become our consistent 'offerings' that become more and more ingrained within the mind. The brain, being neuroplastic, even changes physically to accommodate our belief systems. The problem is that beliefs are innately limited as they are solely based on past events and historic experience. This gives our conditioned thoughts the power to drag us *out* of the present moment hindering our ability to fully experience the unique NOW moments. The mind is the springboard for the creation of our own worlds and although dipping mentally into the past and future tenses can be useful for growth, it is of maximum benefit to us when they are used as references to *supplement* present experience - not to replace them. The present moment is where the greatest opportunity for growth lies and it is also where historic cycles can be broken in order to allow innovation and creativity. The present moment is where success and a new, healthier, happier way of being is found.

When it comes to our sense of being or the direction in which we take our lives, whether we feel good or bad, happy or sad, it is all dependent upon our ability to balance this process of selecting high quality thoughts and residing in the present moment. Every discovery, every work of art, every invention, every innovation we see around us has come from a single, creative, present-moment, *high-quality* thought which gained enough momentum to actualise.

> *'Whether you think you can or whether*
> *you think you can't, you are right'*
> *- Henry Ford*

Our minds are heavily responsible for the differences in our success levels, our varying levels of health and the quality of our relationships. The mind regulates and enhances the stories that we tell ourselves about the meanings of our life experience until our life experiences *become* the meanings that we have assigned. This occurs as the mind attempts to serve its primary objective – **optimization and efficiency.** When we 'ask' the mind to believe a particular concept (by means our repeated thoughts on the topic), the mind will enhance and streamline that particular thought process. Our repeated thoughts turn into what we believe to be *true* about life and the choices we make reflect our beliefs back to us.

Our beliefs can be seen as the '*lens*' through which we project ourselves. These 'lenses' become our paradigms - our way of seeing the world INTO reality. For instance, if you believe that the world is a dark and horrible place to live in, your lens will *hone in* on those aspects of life that validate your argument. If you believe the world is full of opportunity, you will find them everywhere. If you are certain that you will fall over whilst you walk down the street, you will fall. As such, our mind is the *sole determinant* of our lives. It would serve us well to get acquainted with it.

Despite its multiple functions, how the mind works is poorly understood. For instance, modern Science hasn't yet been able to shine much light on the *entire* function of the mind and its capabilities. Many of us are not really aware of how our mind works on a *personal* level nor its impact on the quality of our lives. Mental health disorders such as anxiety and depression are on the rise, without very much advancement in the cure other than medication which often act to brush the deeper issues 'under the carpet'. It is my belief that many of these disorders are symptoms of disconnection – disconnection between the body, mind and the spirit. Through unconscious, programmed patterns of thinking, we have forgotten how to integrate ourselves - to be and feel whole and well - because we are unaware of what the mind, body and spirit are doing in synergy. We have disconnected from our unique, authentic nature which desires expression, resulting in disharmony and dis-ease. There are symptoms of this problem on a more extreme, obvious scale but we may also be suffering from this disconnection on more subtle levels. On a regular basis, we may be choosing thoughts that limit us, the evidence of which may be observable in the undesirable circumstances we find ourselves in and in how *well* we feel.

PAIN IS INEVITABLE BUT SUFFERING IS OPTIONAL ...

Much needless suffering exists even amongst those who appear to 'have it all'. Again, it all boils down to one single factor – our inability to exercise choice and to choose high quality thoughts. When our minds are confined to an old pattern of being and discouraged from expansion, disharmony exists. This disharmony is always caused, at the deepest level, by a fear based, limiting thinking pattern. This limitation creates a limit on our being and we go *against* the flow of life - which is expansive in nature. Authenticity is not readily encouraged by society and education bodies. Often, we are programmed to think alike, to dress alike, to look a particular way and to conform. Above all, we are (consciously or unconsciously) trained to fear going against these standards for fear of rejection. These restrictive patterns of thinking prevent growth, which is then reflected in our well-being.

There has never been a greater need to answer the question *"what leads to sustained happiness, well-being and fulfillment?"* Every single one of our endeavors and every single one of our pursuits holds this question at its core. We are programmed deeply to move towards pleasure and away from pain. This is the goal of every action, no matter which approach is adopted - we ALL want to feel good.

Many of us have learnt how to become reactive to our external and internal environments. This is a disempowering way to function as it takes away our choice. We often use the massive ocean of thoughts that are present within our minds to dictate the course of our lives haphazardly, without sifting through and carefully selecting thoughts which are of benefit to our growth. To some degree, we have lost our mental filters and have learned to react to every stimulus that life offers, using *'tried and tested'*, default methods. It may even be considered a form of mental slavery, addictive and unconscious in its nature. We have placed limits on our *authentic* nature by living a hugely mentally regulated life, shutting ourselves off from the deep, pure wisdom that is held inside the body. This goes against our authenticity and innate desire to grow. How many of us unknowingly ride the waves of fear-based thoughts because it is the way we have always operated? Do you worry excessively about the future or the past? Do you worry about fitting in? Do you worry about what other people think of you? Are you aware of what drives you? What is your WHY? Is it love or is it fear? How many of us really understand where our thoughts and beliefs have come from? Do they even belong to you or have you just picked them up? Are they even relevant anymore? How many of us have actually looked to *see*?

It is quite clear that of the 60,000 or so thoughts and stimuli that we are exposed to each day, *not* all of them will be of benefit to our well-being. Not all of them will direct our lives in a positive way. Not all of them belong to us. Not all of them are relevant. Not all of them lead to happiness and not all of them are anything other than observations and 'noise' from our external environments. Yet *all* of them make their way into our minds. It is no wonder that in the midst of this plethora of thought, without a selection criterion in place, we feel out of control, fearful, confused, unhappy and disempowered. Without a selection process in place that uses the body, we stay stuck within the confines of the mind and fulfilment, joy, happiness, peace, love and success are not possible.

It is, however, important to give the mind the respect it truly deserves and to recognise its power - the mind is HIGHLY efficient. If we suffer a burn to our hand as a child, for instance, we will not need to learn the lesson again and again by going through the exact same process repeatedly. We will immediately detect the source of danger and takes steps towards removing ourselves from the situation, 'bypassing' the direct experience which could potentially be harmful. Uncontrolled and without awareness of its activity, the mind may even make us fear *any* form of heat all together using the above example. The mind recognizes what is required for our personal safety and without direction, can go into a hypersensitivity and 'high alert' for potential danger as well as that which even *remotely* resembles the perceived threat. This is all the mind knows and it will fight tooth and nail to ensure the body is preserved and safe, even if the justification is questionable. Whatsoever makes the body feel 'bad' (whether it be physically or emotionally) will be recognized and remembered by the mind and triggered when deemed appropriate. Stimulated often enough (physically or emotionally) and the mind catalyses the formation of a new neuronal pathway in the brain for 'easy access' to the solution for the only problem it ever has – personal safety.

It bypasses multiple mental steps to get to the outcome but when left to its own devices, the mind will often bypass logic and reason. Although efficient at being on the 'look out', the mind has a tendency to lose its ability to discern. For instance, you may even see the word FIRE and the same alarm bells may start ringing in your mind, warning you of the pain you experienced to your hand. In this way, the mind is a master at survival and therefore of *great* value to us when REAL danger is present. It is not however best suited to understand what real, life threatening danger actually is. The problem is, that the mind learns to see threats to our existence in multiple layers of our lives that are not necessarily life threatening or harmful but are just based on historic memory. These memories - which predominantly *exist* only within the mind space - can cause a huge amount of fear to develop, especially when repeatedly triggered. Often the things we fear are actually the very things that help us to expand and achieve our desires but the pendulum has swung to the opposite pole, and we have learnt to avoid pain 'at all cost', not recognizing that pain is *essential* for our growth. It is how the greatest lessons are learnt. This shows again how the minds' ability to discern and its reliability is questionable...but questioning is crucial to well-being.

One example of the minds inability to discern is when we hold unhealthy beliefs about whether or not we *fit in* to society. The mind may encourage us, based on this belief, to look, accumulate or behave in a certain way. This fear of not being accepted, when stimulated over time, has the ability to form an ingrained *conviction* that, unless we conform, we will not be accepted as our authentic selves. This leads to the fear of <u>not being worthy or the threat of not being loved</u> and, therefore, a perceived sense of danger. This perceived threat to *two* of our basic human needs becomes reinforced over time and dictates aspects of our being. We build barriers and alter our authentic selves in order to avoid 'danger' and perceived pain. The opposing, healthier perspective would be the belief that we are all *unique* and a belief that encourages personal expression but the 'unconscious' mind may hone in on the self-deprecating thoughts based *purely* on habit. This manner of thinking can become crippling unless we increase our *awareness* and select empowering thoughts to build momentum on. The mind in this sense is a very efficient 'watch dog' which, in itself, has obvious benefits but without 'training', the mind has the ability to become *hyper* alert. It is my belief that this 'hyper alert' state and our ingrained fears are responsible for ALL forms of *dis-ease*.

Our basic needs include the need to feel safe, significant, connected and loved, to have stability and variety - yet all around us are messages that make us feel the contrary. From messages on billboards, to what we see on the news, to the stories we are told throughout our lives - we unconsciously *adopt* these messages and our minds act to serve their existence. The good news is that we all have the innate ability to become more *aware* and to understand our minds. This means that we have *choice*.

We hinder ourselves in the psychological *decision making* processes. We defeat ourselves by living life *unconsciously* and unaware of our minds. We defeat ourselves by not giving our mind the attention it deserves – by not loving it and nurturing it. The first thing we need to do in order to become powerful creators of our lives is to consider the notion that we are *more* than just highly efficient programs and from there we can transition into 'waking up' and becoming more *conscious*.

Chapter 2

The function of the Mind

*'If you correct your mind, the rest of
your life will fall into place'*
- Lao Tsu

In the previous chapter we discussed the impact of our thoughts on our personal realities. We discussed how they shape our minds, our beliefs and our circumstances. We also discussed how the quality of our thoughts influence our success levels. Recognising the significance of our thoughts and mastering them can seem a daunting challenge. How do we take charge of our thinking and our realities? How do we *rewire* ourselves for success? The answer lies in understanding how the mind works.

One of the functions of the mind is to TRANSLATE energy

Everything in life is energy in motion. All that our senses are able to detect has an energetic configuration or pattern that the mind translates and gives meaning to. For instance, when we eat an apple, what we are actually tasting at a quantum level is a specific arrangement of <u>electric</u> and <u>magnetic</u> energy held together with the help of particles. It is in the *arrangement* of these energetic bonds that the apple is tasted and identified. The <u>forces</u> that connect the particles together is what we taste, not the particles themselves. In this example, the mind translates the energy within the food, processes it and absorbs it into its own energy field.

The same principle applies to the hearing of sound, the sensation of touch, seeing, smelling and intuitive guidance. The mind detects *vibration* (which ALL particles are continuously in the process of), and the knock on effect of that vibration on the physical senses, creating its own interpretation of life. This is how *every* aspect of our external environment is experienced and how energy makes its way into our mind and physical space.

When we look at a stationary object, we see it as solid and rigid through our senses. On a microscopic level however, the atoms - the building blocks - do not even touch each other. They are held together by means of this invisible, electromagnetic force, forming the structure of the perceived object that has been formed through layers and layers of energy. Furthermore, all atoms that make up *any* object are approximately 99.9% space, hardly any of it is matter, yet they have the ability to form something that appears to be quite the opposite of empty space. Even our bodies are predominantly 'empty' yet we see fully functioning, solid form. It is said that if all of the *actual* substance within our body were to be condensed, it would be the size of a mere pinhead! There is virtually *zero* substance to anything that we are able to see, feel, touch, smell or hear. All of matter is almost entirely energy in motion.

Our human senses are innately limited. As you are reading this book for instance, it may be difficult to imagine that you are travelling hundreds and thousands of miles *per second* through space, whilst physically feeling 'stillness'. The mind also has the ability to further distort energy vibration once processed by the senses through emotional attachment. For example, if a certain song reminds you of a difficult time in your life, hearing the song - even decades down the line - can cause the resurfacing of emotions linked to those events. This association can alter the way in which the song is perceived as a whole. Even if the song is composed to meet perfect musical standards, you may feel discomfort and dislike the experience of listening due to its emotional significance. In itself, the minds ability to detect energy and translate it does not create variations in perspective but its ability to add *meaning* does. This can lead to the existence of multiple perspectives, beliefs and opinion i.e. versions of reality amongst individuals. For this reason, reality is sometimes considered an illusion, Maya, due to the fluid nature of energy, the limitation of our senses, the massive variation in mental interpretations and the significant emotional associations of the human experience.

Every aspect of life is held in balance by means of energetic interaction, the invisible force. What we see as distinguished separation between form is not separation at all. Even our skin is not solid at a cellular or quantum level. Energy courses through every aspect of the Universe connecting it by an invisible, energetic 'blueprint' or 'web' upon which the varying forms of life are suspended and layered in energetic dimensions practising perfect balance. This electromagnetic background grid is the only constant within this fluid reality and is the backbone of all existence. Understanding the mind means understanding that it translates a very limited aspect of this vast energetic spectrum.

There is more to life than meets the eye. Our physical eyes only have the ability to see 1% of the entire electromagnetic spectrum. We cannot see the ultraviolet light that a bumble bee does when it hovers from flower to flower. We cannot see X-rays, microwaves or even effectively in the dark. We cannot hear the high pitched noises that a dog can hear. Elephants can detect the call of another from 3 miles away and are even reported to detect changes in the environment prior to an earthquake. Their versions of reality are *very* different to ours even though they represent a tiny aspect of the entire Universe. Nothing that we experience through our 5 senses is as it seems, yet we often believe with <u>complete conviction</u> that our individual beliefs, realities, opinions and perceptions are the *complete* representation of what is true and what is not. In this sense, what is 'real' is subject to such a huge amount of interpretation that reality is virtually impossible to define.

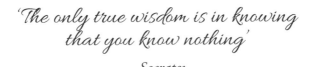

*'The only true wisdom is in knowing
that you know nothing'*

- Socrates

Although we can use certain laws and principles that are based on repeatable and predictable results (i.e. the pursuits of Science) to help us define how life operates - these processes can be limited due to their foundations being set only on historic experience. Science can prove certain aspects of life but not the whole picture. The only *undeniable* reality is that of the underlying energetic 'grid' unlike the realities created by the mind.

This grid or energetic field is a highly coordinated, mathematically precise <u>blueprint</u> that lies beneath *all* form – almost like cosmic glue holding the entire Universe together. In order to positively influence our lives, it is far more powerful and profound to create ripples of influence at the core level of existence, at the level of **energy**. Being equipped with (a) the awareness that the mind is a separate entity to us (b) the knowledge of how this powerful translator of energy works and (c) recognition of the influence we have on this field by our thoughts and emotions - it may be clear to see how much of an evolutionary advantage we have and desire to exercise it. Understanding the principles of energy and our individual, profound impact on the blueprint, prevents needless suffering caused by the failed attempts at changing our versions of reality from the outside, from the superficial layers.

Not my will, Higher will be done.

These cycles of trying to change our reality from any place *other* than from the level of the blueprint, can be compared to removing the raw ingredients of a cake *after* it has been baked. It is not totally impossible but significantly arduous. By understanding the impact of working at the **core** level of form, we can create sustained and dependable change in our lives. By working on ourselves, the energy of our thoughts and by understanding how powerful our emotions are, we can learn how to 'manipulate' energy to create Higher Minded positive change. This manner of bringing about change is fulfilling, expansive in nature and deeply empowering.

Second function: The mind not only translates but also EMITS energy into its surroundings via our bodies and out into the external environment.

We are *constantly* emitting and radiating energy, the most powerful of which are our emotions which are fuelled by the thoughts that occur within the mind. Thoughts and emotions create *tangible* changes within the body, from fluctuations in temperature and heart rate to physical changes in the tissues. Emotions that stem from fear cause an overall <u>contraction</u> in our energy output which leads to changes such as contraction in our muscles and our posture, and an increase in our heart rate for example. Feeling love however <u>expands</u> our energy, causing effects such as the expansion of our chests and the reduction in heart rate. These internal changes in turn, impact our external environment which, as mentioned previously, are not separate due to energetic fluidity that exists between all things.

A thought is a physical movement within the body that can build enough momentum to create an emotional response. Over time, this can lead to changes in the physical body and our external environments. The best way to influence the mind is to acknowledge and use these emotional, physical and external responses to identify the thoughts that are in operation. Similarly, the best way to influence our *external* environments is to create at the level of thought. For this reason, strong connection to our bodies and our emotions leads to the intelligence that is required to identify and direct our thoughts and our lives. The trouble is that often trauma and pain from the past can lead to disconnection between our mind, our body and our emotions. This occurs in order to avoid feeling massive pain which we are deeply programmed to avoid. We can shut ourselves off from feeling all together. This disconnection leads to further suffering, limitation on our expansion and a cap on our levels of fulfilment.

Our thoughts create major ripples in the energetic web of life. We have the ability to channel thought towards favourable circumstances. When we understand how the mind works and when we know what we want, we can become *deliberate* creators instead of being influenced by the external stimuli of life. By influencing the energy of our desires, we are able to impact form at the most fundamental level. Like a snowball, sustaining the momentum of desirable thoughts and emotions will eventually lead to guaranteed action, outcome and manifestation. Acting towards our desires is not the primary step in creation - the thinking and emotional energies need to marry first. Those who merely act without emotional and energetic integrity, often find that they struggle to fulfil their desires and if they do, they struggle to maintain them.

The energetic marriage between thought, emotion and action in order to actualise our desires is also known as manifestation. Manifestation can help us or hinder us based on the thoughts we practice most often – negative or positive, energetically contracting or energetically expanding. Also known as KARMA. If this sounds like a difficult process to master, you should know that if you have the ability to think, you have been carrying out this process your entire life. We have been influencing the field of potential *consistently* by our thoughts and emotions - the manifestations of which, by means of quantum law, we see all around us. This is how powerful each one of us is in our creative abilities. To change our circumstances from undesirable to desirable is not that difficult. It involves the exact same process we are used to but directed in a different way. We just need to become more **aware** of what exactly it is that we are manifesting.

The advancement of technology and the overall advancements of mankind have been manifested in the same way, by the channeling of thought towards ideas, dreams and goals, until they have materialised. *Everything* we see around us is the manifestation of form via the sustained, channeled energy of thought.

The mind is also a highly efficient and a well regulated storage system and has the capacity to store huge quantities of information. In fact, it does not forget a thing. As mentioned in the previous chapter, our minds are efficient accumulators of our internal and external, current and historic experiences, our perceptions and our interpretations. We have access to an *endless* supply of 'translated' and stored energy that gives us a huge number of options to select our mental 'direction' from, on a day to day, minute to minute, second to second basis. In the absence of a decision making process, however, we can also feel confused and suffer from information overload. Unless we recognise the power we have over a mental 'sifting' process, this information overload can lead to fear, stress, anxiety, helplessness, burnout and a whole host of negative emotions. We can feel depression and despair whilst we wade through the confusion of the mind, *habitually* selecting the thoughts that are self-deprecating or fear based in nature. Empowerment is recognising that you are in control of which thoughts you choose to pay attention to and that you *always* have a choice. Mastering this art leads to a profound level of freedom and the deep understanding that the mind is best suited when it is of service to you – not when it acts as an authority.

When we select a particular thought to pay attention to, whether it be consciously or unconsciously, a domino effect is created. The thought gains energy by finding more thoughts that are similar in nature from the plethora of thoughts that are available in the mind. The initial thought expands and gains momentum – an innate *desire* and characteristic of energy in general. Unless interrupted, this process (in the fertile 'soil' of our minds) is sustained and self-perpetuating. One single thought can build enough energy and momentum to not only affect our emotions, our body and our biochemistry but also our circumstances and our lives. The minds ability to store such vast quantities of information can give us choice but can also hinder us unless we *consciously* direct it. Unless we master it.

Not only will sustained thoughts on a particular topic lead to internal and external change, they will also create physical changes in the brain. Consistent thinking patterns lead to altered brain wave patterns, the formation of new neuronal pathways and the reconfiguration of brain tissue. This makes it even *more* efficient at what it does – and what it does is to listen to orders! The brain physically rewires itself in order to optimise the regular thinking patterns based on what the brain is 'commanded' to do. Our thoughts can literally change our brain and our body.

A fear-based 'selection process' is what many of us are programmed to adopt from a young age. The threat to our survival, acceptance and fulfilment is consistently emphasised by the media, our education authorities, the government, multi-million dollar industries who profit from us thinking in this way and sometimes even those who care about us - like our well-wishing parents, friends and relatives. The inability to discern creates *imbalance* on an individual and on a global scale. Our survival instincts are constantly sensitized through these avenues and as a result we have become efficient at 'boxing ourselves in' to an emotional *safe zone*. Staying in this confined place, we go against our natural desire to grow and expand *with* the Universe. This discord, this contraction, creates energetic dis-ease within us, which presents itself as emotional, physical, mental and spiritual problems. It is my belief that this discord is the *major* root cause of virtually all of the suffering we see in the world.

Although we may not have complete control over our external environments, we do have control over our internal environment. The mastery of *this* environment leads to inevitable change in the external and creates a ripple effect that impacts the entire energetic field that we are all an integral part of. This not only positively impacts our lives but it also helps to balance the *Yin* and *Yang* energies – the contracting and expanding energies of the planet.

The key to mastering our thoughts, our internal environment and our lives is to recognise that **you are not your thoughts**. They are comparable to *possessions* we have accumulated and attached ourselves to over time. The mere fact that we have the ability to sit back, close our eyes and consciously *watch* the contents of our minds and our thoughts in action, suggests that there is *another* aspect of ourselves that is observing. It points to a deeper layer of ourselves being in operation. Being in this energetically *detached* state allows us to analyse and question the validity of our thinking habits and direct them for our own benefit.

You are the awareness beneath thought, which means that your thoughts can not define you. Just like a body part cannot define who you are, a thought, a belief or a conviction cannot either. They are very much separate, superficial and external to your real *core* self. Success comes from understanding this principle and from detaching from our thoughts enough to see them in operation. Awareness is the *primary* step in the sifting, sorting and selection of beneficial thought, to channel towards our desires. Detachment from our thoughts allows us to see with *clarity* and to consciously select the direction of our mind. When we attach who we are to our thoughts and *identify* with them i.e. make them responsible for our identity, we are directed *by* them. When we detach from our thoughts, we are back in the driver's seat of our lives. We harness authentic power by creating *space* between our observing mind and our thinking mind. By refining this art, you are no longer a victim and you become a conscious creator of your destiny. The ability to observe thought is a form of meditation - a heightened state of awareness. This process helps to take us back to our core self and puts us back in charge of our physical realities. This form of personal power is authentic, magnetic and *influential* and has its foundation firmly built on positive *internal* influence.

Chapter 3

We have two voices

An old Cherokee is teaching his grandson about life.

"A fight is going on inside me," he said to the boy. "It is a terrible fight and it is between two wolves. One is evil – he is anger,

envy, sorrow, regret, greed, arrogance, self-pity, guilt, resentment, inferiority,

lies, false pride, superiority, and ego."

He continued, "The other is good – he is joy, peace, love, hope, serenity, humility,

kindness, benevolence, empathy, generosity, truth, compassion, and faith. The

same fight is going on inside you – and inside every other person, too."

The grandson thought about it for a minute and then asked his grandfather,

"Which wolf will win?"

The old Cherokee simply replied, "The one you feed.

We all have two 'wolves' – or two *voices*. Which voice we choose to nurture has the greatest impact on our lives, our well-being, our emotional states, our relationships, our success levels and, at the most quantum level, the electromagnetic field generated by the body often referred to as the *aura*. The aura strongly reflects our emotional states and extends beyond the physical body creating a tangible impact on our surroundings whether we are aware of it or not. When our emotional state and energetic output is of *high* vibration i.e. when we feel the most loving or when we feel the happiest, our aura can expand out to fill an entire room.

'High' and 'Low' vibration are terms used to describe the characteristics of energy. Energy travels in waves between 2 extremes:

- Shortest in wavelength and fast - **HIGH** vibration, or
- Longest in wavelength and slow - **LOW** vibration.

The lower the vibration, the denser the energy is. A table is made up of atoms connected by energy vibrating at a much *lower* vibration than water for instance, which has a much higher overall vibration making it lighter and more fluid than the denser table. Meat has a denser energy vibration than fruit, making fruit a 'higher vibrational' food.

The spectrum of our emotions are also of varying vibrational frequency. Being in love for example emits energy of higher vibration than being depressed - which emits a lower, denser vibration. The differing emotional states that we are in have a significant impact on the quality of our mental and physical states, our aura and our relationship with our surroundings. The higher our vibration, the more energetic we feel and the greater our capacity to influence our environment, near and far. The quality of our aura becomes more energetically cohesive when we are in loving, excitable states - which, as you will see throughout the course of the book, make us extremely powerful and magnetic: the backbone qualities of a potent state known as *charisma*.

Our energy field is connected to and *overlays* the background field that makes life possible. Almost like the layers of an onion. It is a well-known fact of quantum science that the slightest movement within our physical field creates an energetic impact on the entire underlying web. Our energetic influence, in the form of thought, emotion and action, is like tugging one of the corners of this infinitely large energetic blanket. The tiniest movement of one aspect, impacts the whole. When we move, even at the most atomic level, even via a thought, we affect the field at every possible point. Our emotions and actions, which have a very strong influence on the field, affect the field with even greater intensity. We interact with *everything* around us, all of the time, whether we realise it or not – people, situations and this sea of underlying energy. The higher our vibration, the greater the fluidity and impact of our energy and the greater its influence on the web of life.

As within, so without.

As a result of this deep connection, we have the ability to influence and be influenced by each other and our external environments. Any energetic change within ourselves, including our thoughts, will impact the *entire* cosmos at the most fundamental level. Any energetic change in the cosmos will impact us at the most basic level. The importance of this potent *'field'* has been emphasized by virtually every culture from around the world - from modern day findings going back thousands of years – with references to it and its sacred geometry in and around ancient carvings, diagrams and ancient text.

Due to our ability to consciously, through emotion and thought, influence the field, we are incredibly powerful. Every thought creates a *measurable* electromagnetic wave that is perceivable on subtle levels. The mind is the *catalyst* and the most crucial, underlying determinant of our influence as it sets off a chain reaction impacting our emotions and actions. It is, therefore, of extreme value to recognise and understand the major players – the two voices - that exist within the mind.

So what are these forces - the two voices?

One of these voices is referred to as the **Ego**. The Ego is loud, manages and assesses risk, takes on board and logically organises past information, forms our identity based on experience and has an innate tendency to <u>fear</u>, constantly looking out for risks to our survival and for methods of preservation. It places great significance on all of our accumulations - including our thoughts, beliefs, ideas and possessions, which it relies upon to form our identity. The Ego can be extremely useful in life threatening situations where plenty of information and 'tried and tested' safety measures are warranted to increase our chance of survival, but in those who have an overactive, hypersensitised, triggered or overstimulated Ego, symptoms related to chronic fear can develop. We use the term 'egotistical' often. An egotistical person displays <u>false</u> confidence and an unhealthy attachment to some 'thing' - whether it be a thought, belief, possession or identity, in order to compensate for a lack of self-worth. In the traditional sense, an egotistical person, fundamentally displays symptoms of fear – the fear of not being accepted or being worthy without some form of 'accumulation'. An overactive Ego mind, however, is not limited to this definition only and can relate to *any* expression of fear, such as aggression, worry, anxiety and frustration. In this sense, fear – which stems from the Ego mind – expresses itself in multiple different ways despite being commonly associated with a form of arrogance.

At the most basic level, the Ego seeks to keep us safe and out of danger. The basis of its rationale lie in historic experience and it perceives all and any painful events as potentially 'dangerous' in nature, including the emotionally painful ones. These events can involve those we have directly experienced or even those which we have learned of. *Anything* with a negative emotional attachment can become a reason for the Ego to come into play. In any given situation that is considered by the Ego to be a potential threat to physical or emotional survival, it will draw out information from the past - a whole host of thoughts, memories, justifications and experiences - in order to analyse the risk and prevent the undertaking of a particular 'harmful' action. A mental 'case' is prepared, highlighting the risks and heeding the warnings. This process of case making may not be instigated by a physical threat necessarily (for which the Ego mind is best suited) but can also include emotional threats, such as the threat of disconnection from others or a threat to receiving love and acceptance – both of which are basic human needs. When there is a threat to these emotional needs being met, the Ego can also come back into operation. Due to its bolshie nature, the Ego demands to make its concerns known to you and can be the loudest, most dominant voice in our heads. In genuinely dangerous situations, the Ego is perfectly suited and of huge benefit to us but when the threat is not necessarily life threatening, the Ego often has a 'Bull in a China shop' approach.

Effectively, whenever we think any fear based thoughts, the Ego is in play. It is a highly evolved, 2-million-year old <u>tool</u> that is concerned, solely, with survival of itself and you, its 'carrier'. As with everything *other* than the observational witness within ourselves, the Ego mind is very much a separate entity to our core self. Any event that validates its need to be in operation will enhance its existence and the more validation it gets, the stronger and more influential it becomes. Like all forms of energy, unless interrupted, it can build a tremendous momentum. It is one of the strongest forces that is in operation in existence and unless balanced through the light of awareness, it has the ability to steer our lives towards chronic fear based living.

The Ego is admirably and extremely intelligent, efficient and powerful. When it is not operating in harmony with our entire being however, suffering exists. When we look around us we may recognise ways in which an imbalanced and a hypersensitive Ego can be validated and further enhanced by its surroundings. This can include advertisements for cosmetic products for instance, which can feed the fear of not being enough, to the feelings of inadequacy in the presence of someone who is seemingly more successful than you are, or feelings of insignificance or aggression if someone looks at you funny. Often the Ego, with its assumptions based on fear, attempts to make *any* external situation a potential threat to survival or our human needs and therefore demands we pay regular attention to it. Not only does this take a huge amount of focus, it is also energetically draining and limits our experience of life. In fact, in the vast majority of circumstances, complete focus on the Ego dialogue is completely unnecessary.

Sustained fear based emotions stemming from the Ego have the general characteristic of <u>contracting</u> our energy and causing loss of vitality - mentally, physically and energetically - leading to subsequent stagnation of our growth. Fundamentally, the Ego wants to protect us from danger and can become our ally if we learn to manage it. We need to place it, with the respect it deserves, into the passenger seat of our lives and out of the drivers'. Self-mastery relies upon our ability to sift through the continuous stream of unconscious, programmed thoughts in order to eliminate those thoughts that are not *real* threats to our existence but are kept active by the Ego. Personal power surfaces when we learn to use the powerful Ego when it's *really* necessary, rather than it using our energy haphazardly.

It is human nature to avoid pain and seek pleasure. The associations we make with each can either help us to grow and empower us or limit/disempower us. These associations are wired into us based on our experiences and the consistent thoughts that we think about them. These in turn become our beliefs. Being able to detach from these thoughts enough to see them clearly, helps us to create mental associations for *positive* benefit and growth and to clear the ones that do not by default. For instance, if you are looking to get fitter and take up exercise, rather than attaching pain to the physical activity of exercise, you can learn to attach pain to the *lack* of it. By associating pleasure *with* physical exercise and associating pain with its *absence* and by reinforcing these associations, we can use our minds to help us to grow and expand towards that which we desire. For this to happen, we must increase our awareness so we may understand what it is that we attach pain and pleasure to and how our current/past experiences have influenced this process. We need to differentiate between pain that encourages growth, pain that leads to limitation and genuine danger. We can become masters of our lives by learning to <u>discern</u>, by learning to see 'clearly' and by becoming more conscious of our internal dialogue.

The second voice is the deeper voice of the **Heart**. It is the quiet, non-imposing *'magician'* that speaks to us via visceral feeling opposed to mental thought that comes from the surface level of existence. The Hearts' voice offers us nurturing encouragement and profound wisdom. In order to 'hear' it, we must cultivate much deeper listening skills i.e. listening with *every* part of our physical being and not just the Mind. The Mind relies upon past knowledge for its stability, the Heart relies upon present moment wisdom which channels through the body. For this reason, it is important that we are connected to and increase our sensitivity to changes that occur within the body so that it can act almost like a satellite dish waiting for important signals from the Heart. We need to learn to travel outside of the thinking mind and expand our awareness to incorporate our entire being. This is readily observed in young children and animals who live moment to moment, being guided by their feelings and emotions opposed to their logical thought processes.

The voice of the Heart lives in the present moment. It is the opposing lovebased energy of the Ego – the opposite end of the same 'pole'. What this means is that when a fear based thought is in operation the opposing Heart based feeling is always accessible and nearby. Understanding this can help us to shift from Ego based thought to Heart based wisdom – moving us out of lower vibrational, disempowering states and into higher vibrational, empowering states instead. Learning to listen to the Hearts' voice allows us to build energetic momentum on Heart based present moment wisdom, which guides us to our joys and passions. The *merging* of the Ego voice with Heart centred wisdom is the aim, so that neither is rejected and both can be utilised when best suited. This enables us to move towards our passions in a way that avoids *actual* harm.

The Hearts' voice does not fear and offers wisdom, encouragement, courage and self-esteem - contrary to the wary Ego. When nurtured and balanced against the Ego, the voice of the Heart is our greatest friend. It is humble in its approach and does not demand attention like the boisterous Ego does. Instead the Heart patiently waits for you to tune into it. By moving from Ego to Heart, from thinking to feeling, from a negative to a positive mind set, we raise our energetic vibration enough to tune into even higher forms of intelligent vibration such as intuition, creativity, inspiration and a different level of universal genius.

It only takes for us to study the innate intelligence of the body to gain some idea of the intelligence that these higher forms of energy have. Source intelligence is responsible for the creation of every aspect of nature. When we tune into this intelligence, it predominantly communicates via the Heart, leading to an undeniable *knowingness* and urge to act. This urge can be supported further by the Hearts' continued encouragement whenever you tame the Ego mind and tune in. By paving the way for Heart centred, higher intelligence to emerge, we connect with a flawless form of loving guidance and why, throughout time, we have been encouraged to 'follow our hearts'. This intelligence guides us towards our deep seated desires provided we deliberately and consciously choose which 'voice' to nurture.

There is often a mistaken tendency to want to see the Ego mind as the 'enemy' and quite often people who try to align with their purpose will attack this aspect of their being. We forget that the Ego is there for an important purpose and therefore warrants respect and appreciation. The Ego actually appreciates and mellows in the presence of loving kindness that's directed from within.

Sometimes unknowingly, we tend to give the Ego mind justification and permission to thrive, as we feed it *more* fear in the form of our own fear of its existence and presence. Understanding the Egos' role in justified situations and recognising its value allows for the complete acceptance of that aspect of ourselves. After all, accepting the Ego is true wholeness, acceptance of who you are and a form of unconditional love directed at yourself. This is the foundation of *all* forms of unconditional love. Resisting the Ego acts to empower it into further imbalance. Once we appreciate it and accept it for what it is, the Ego mind takes a 'back seat' and operates as a peaceful, useful ally and emerges in the presence of actual danger. It then does not feel the need to demand attention all of the time.

The merging of the Ego with Heart centred wisdom and the harmonious combination of the two innate energies, act to cultivate a powerfully expansive and extremely intelligent driving force which creates ripples throughout the aura. The key to moving towards our passions is to use this force and to unidentify from the Mind, following through on the feelings that are Heart centred opposed to Ego based. The Ego can thereafter be utilised to <u>carry out</u> the practical steps for which it is best suited, as an operator. The fusion between Yin and Yang, light and dark, Ego and Soul is true wholeness, self-acceptance and integrity. It provides the fertile soil in which our unique gifts can grow and creates space for higher minded attunement. This is the balance to strive for in order to propel ourselves into expansion and to experience the deep fulfilment that comes with it, and it all comes from the expanded awareness of who and what we are.

"The two wolves in me are not at war. In fact, they are lovers. The black wolf is powerful and reckless and howls at the moon. The white wolf is spiritual and kind and prefers bathing in the sun. They are polar opposites, therefore they are the perfect pair. I feed them both. I control them both"

Chapter 4

What is Consciousness?

In spiritual terms, *Consciousness* is our ability to SEE.

To define the term 'seeing' however is not as simple as it appears. For instance, if you were asked to picture a red car, which aspect of you is it that sees the car in that instant? It's surely not your physical eyes which see what is physically present. Then what is it? What we actually see with when asked to picture the car is a *deeper* form of vision.

The same principle applies if you were asked to visualise something that has never been seen with the physical eyes before – such as a green, luminous, elephant or even possibly your dream life. As can be seen here, *seeing* in the traditional sense using your physical eyes, isn't necessarily the true, *complete* definition of pure vision. It points to alternative forms of vision being available and in operation, a small branch of which being imagination. It also points towards the difficulty in defining the term 'seeing' and what it is that is actually does the 'seeing'. Is it your eyes? Is it something beyond that? How far does the rabbit hole go?

Here I am sitting on my chair typing these words. Looking at the chair, I see it has four legs, a seat, two arms, a cushion and a back rest but if I could see the chair as atoms through a microscope, as elemental, I would see it as vibrating, charged particles held together via energetic bonds and the whole structure of the chair would be predominantly empty space because that is the nature of the component parts. When we look at the night sky, many of the stars that we see do not even exist any longer. What we see is light travelling to our eyes well after the death of the star. In this example the definition of 'seeing' and *what* we are seeing is subject to debate. This highlights the limitation of seeing with our physical eyes and an insight into the spectrum of vision. None of the perspectives of vision are correct or incorrect, good or bad ways of seeing, merely varying degrees of vision from what we call, altered states of consciousness.

"As above, so below. As within, so without"

– Hermes Trismegistus

Every living being, including plants, insects, animals and ourselves, operate from varying degrees of *pure* vision or consciousness, quite like being able to see the chair in the above example from alternate viewpoints. Pure consciousness can be compared to the *broadest* perspective and therefore possessing the ability to see at the most elemental level – at the *purest and deepest* form of reality. Below this level of vision, life operates at varying degrees of consciousness almost like the splitting of white light into the colours of the rainbow, each colour possessing an infinite spectrum in itself. As a result of the various 'forms' that are perceivable, everything exists on *multiple* levels, from physical form through to energetic form. All of these forms exist and they do so simultaneously.

If this theory is to be believed, it also points to expanded and multiple versions of *ourselves* operating in existence too. Varying dimensions and multiple layers with a core, deep truth within us at our core. Pure vision, or pure consciousness, is seeing form at the most energetic level, at its core level, an ability that goes far beyond the means of modern science at this stage of our evolution. Pure consciousness is the highest, most expanded viewpoint - seeing at the level of the energetic blueprint or the highest bird's eye perspective. So the purer and more expanded our consciousness, the closer we are to the background, foundational 'field' of energy that makes life possible and the broader our perspective, which comes with many life altering advantages.

Pure consciousness and the background field of energy are one and the same. They cannot be separated or exist without the other. It is that aspect of life that has *'thought'* the Universe into manifestation; the energy that gave birth to all aspects of life. A field of pure, intelligent, bubbling potential. Just as some *'thing'* cannot be formed from NO *'thing'*, the Universe cannot be formed from a complete lack of existence. It exists as a result of a greater level of consciousness – one that is of pure potential – a

Divine 'spark' and a force of energy. Call it the Big Bang, call it Pure Consciousness, call it a thought – the principle is the same – everything arises when lightning strikes pure potential. Furthermore, the process that thought the Universe into reality is the exact same process we adopt when we put thought into action. In essence, the more creative potential we have, the greater and broader our level of consciousness. The more expanded our level of consciousness, the greater our creative potential. Our thoughts are the potential, the ignition, that ignite creativity and lead to creation on a personal level and it is thought, stemming from a *higher* mind, that leads to creation on a Universal level. The difference in our creative potential lies in our ability to 'see' based on how conscious we are and therefore our ability to connect with the Universal field.

Where a lioness may operate solely from the level of consciousness that drives her to hunt, we may be able to operate from this primal level of consciousness as well as from the level that makes us feel compassion for the prey. These are just two differing levels of consciousness that we as humans can expand and contract into – one is just a broader perspective than the other. As we learn to see from broader or higher perspective, we 'ascend' up the ladder of consciousness. Technically, it is less of an ascension up and more of an expansion into our broader, more elemental form. There are in reality *infinite* levels of consciousness and therefore infinite forms of infinite aspects of the Universe that are in operation. So long as the Universe continues to expand exponentially, this will always be the case.

'*Everything you can imagine is real*'
- Pablo Picasso

This ability that we have to become aware, grow and alter our levels of consciousness is what makes us powerful as human beings. Our ability to raise our personal vibration (through the deliberate choosing of thoughts that lead to more loving emotional states) and the subsequent ability to have broader minded perspective is linked to our success on all levels. This *limitless* potential for the expansion of our consciousness is what enables us to see and **THINK** our versions of reality into existence. Whether they are desirable or not, the system if the same – expansion of our consciousness to visualise and create our reality. The positive nurturing of our emotions is what leads to the creation of desirable circumstances in our lives. This is the core principle adopted by some of the most successful people on the planet. Those that are able to create and fulfil their desires have understood the significance of emotional mastery, creative visualisation, broader minded perspective and have attached energetic 'fuel' to the process through the building of momentum on high quality thoughts. Knowingly or unknowingly, consciously or unconsciously, these are the steps that you use to underpin **EVERY** creative process you undergo which is based on a vision stemming from broader minded perspective. The broader the perspective, or the more expanded our levels of consciousness, the greater the vision and the greater our capacity to influence our realities.

In spiritual terms, being conscious is more than just the ability to have differing perspectives or viewpoints. It is also a deep connection to the field of pure potentiality and the 'tuning in' to its properties. This connection to the field, also known as Source energy, cultivates an innate knowingness and awareness of reality, or 'truth' that we all possess at the most fundamental level. This connection also allows us to draw upon the energy and qualities of the field including its creative, inspirational essence.

The reason why we as souls pass from lifetime to lifetime is in an attempt to evolve and reach this heightened state of pure consciousness; to reconnect with our Source energy and to remember who we truly are. It is not a reaching in fact, it is more of a 'stripping back' to get to our core essence. The Souls' energy, like any form of energy, can never be destroyed – it only ever changes form and depending on the vibration of our energy and our emotional states, we will have the ability to 'strip back' rapidly or slowly revealing more of our Souls' light.

The way we incarnate into human form can be compared to the formation of a crystallised ice cube, which has a physically dense, tangible vibration. Source energy can be compared to steam – the most fluid, most *expanded* state. Aspects of Source energy crystallise into form, including those aspects that contain our 'accumulated' vibrations across lifetimes, giving us our physical, unique human existence. These vibrations are never destroyed only altered as we transition between lifetimes. We effectively 'bring down' our varying vibrational states for the purposes of expression and further transmutation leading to expansion.

Unlike the ice cube, however, we have been gifted with the ability that we can alter our vibrational states by the deliberate adjustment of our thoughts and emotions. Our energy is made 'denser' through negative emotion, which always stem from fear and can be made 'lighter' through positive emotion. We can be the ice cube, the water and the steam at the flick of a thought. The denser our personal vibration, the more hindered is our growth, literally 'weighing' us down energetically. Positive, loving emotion on the other hand raises our vibration, placing us in and connecting us to expanded, altered, more conscious and creative states.

Our life experiences mirror our emotional and vibrational states. The closer we are to vibrating at the same frequency as Source, the greater our ability to expand, to create and make powerful, positive influence in our lives – just like Source energy does. Pure consciousness is referred to as Truth with a capital 'T' as it is the purest form of vision and seeing. It is a crystal clear form of clarity of 'all that is', not only from the deepest quantum level but also from the highest, most 'birds eye' and, by default, the *truest* perspective. Pure consciousness (Source energy) encompasses all perspectives and all forms. When our limited consciousness merges with that which is infinite, pure consciousness, it is referred to as <u>Enlightenment</u> – a state of seeing with pure clarity, a state of pure creativity, connectivity, oneness with and seeing the perfection of the 'whole'.

It is useful to know that it is only ever in the absence of clarity that we feel powerless, confused and disempowered. The greater our levels of consciousness (and therefore clarity), the more empowered we feel. It is difficult to feel stressed, depressed or anxious about things that you have maximum clarity over, clarity moves you out of stagnation to flow *with* the natural current of the Universe. It is therefore of paramount importance to our wellbeing that we free ourselves via the pursuit of the expansion of our consciousness.

Shine your **LIGHT**.

Understanding that we have certain limits on our consciousness helps to keep our minds open to the possibility of more and allows room for growth. Unless we expand our consciousness beyond our limited perspectives, thoughts and beliefs and release our attachments to them, it is impossible to see the Divine, perfect order of all that occurs within our lives. Without seeing this, without learning to see outside the 'box', we feel powerless, uninspired, limited, stagnant and hopeless. When we connect to something greater than our limited self-i.e. our *Higher* Selves, we set off a chain reaction to deepen our connection to Source. Life becomes full of possibility, guidance, wisdom, unconditional love and creativity. Our lives become *infused* with the qualities of Source energy itself.

The reason why the varying degrees of consciousness exist in the first place, is for two major reasons:

The first function is for **EXPANSION**.

Source energy is responsible for the creation of the entire Universe and all forms of life. It is the underlying layer of energy holding all form together. In order for the Universe to expand, which it does so constantly and exponentially, we have *separated* from this energetic 'pool' of pure consciousness and this separation exists in varying degrees, along an infinite spectrum. Picture splatting paint onto a canvas with different aspects of the paint spreading out in varying shapes, quantities and distances from the original impact. This initial separation is responsible for the emotions of fear and the lack of power that we may feel, depending on the degree of our separation. The most extreme end of the separation is often termed the 'Alpha' and unity with pure consciousness is often termed the 'Omega'. They are both different facets, the opposing energies of the same whole with life existing between the two.

This may lead you to ask the question - *how does separation lead to expansion?* It may even sound somewhat cruel to be torn away from a loving creator to be forced into experiencing these perceived negative states.

In order to answer 'why', picture a bow and an arrow. In order for the arrow to propel forwards, it needs to be pulled back i.e. there needs to be separation of the string from the actual bow. The further back the arrow on the bow is pulled, the further forwards the arrow will go. This analogy describes the contracting and expanding, macro and microcosmic infinite cycles of creation and therefore the overall expansive nature of the Universe. Everything that expands is balanced against an equal and opposite force. Spiritually speaking, this is the role of difficult (contracting) emotional times and feelings of disconnection in our evolution. The purpose was never to stay in a contracted place, but to use periods of disconnection (and their associated fear based symptoms) to move forwards with greater intensity. To expand *with* the Universe and our true nature. Those who are considered to be 'offensive' in their actions or whom so ever appear to create perceived problems in the world are actually playing their role of separation to an extreme level - and dare I say it, for the overall expansion and the 'greater good' of collective growth. From a higher perspective, the varying degrees of separation are never judged as 'good' or 'bad' they are just seen as important component parts of the bigger picture. So is every single individual, event and aspect of their life. Source is unconditional love with an emphasis on **GROWTH**.

The difficulty is that staying stuck in an emotionally separated state is encouraged in many ways from a third dimensional, human perspective. Society, mass media, our various upbringings, pain and suffering and many external factors 'keep' us in this separated state whilst we are unaware and unconscious of the roles that the smaller component parts play in the overall picture.

As well as this, many energetic forces play a role in influencing expansion. In reality there is no 'good' or 'bad', 'right' or 'wrong', there is only expansion and contraction and their differing properties and scales. To those who are 'unconscious', different aspects of life encourage them to stay stuck in a separated state which often manifests as suffering on some level, whether it be physical, emotional or spiritual. This was not the original intention behind the initial separation and the challenges we face. This is why we have been equipped with the Ego mind to help us navigate safely back to our powerful selves at the centre of our being, where we connect with Source. The Ego serves to avoid danger and should be used as a tool but it often gets extremely stimulated. As a result we have misinterpreted and given its function far too much importance, which can keep us stuck in separation unless we can learn how to use the Ego in the way it was intended - from a place of Soul empowerment and not Ego empowerment. Unfortunately, many of us have learnt to live in sustained states of fear and this stops us from expanding. This chronic state of separation that many people suffer from bleeds into how they feel about themselves, others and the world at large and has a direct impact on the quality of their lives.

The second purpose of this wide spectrum of consciousness is for Source energy to **EXPERIENCE ITSELF**.

> *'We are not a human being having a spiritual experience, we are spiritual beings having a human experience'*
>
> **- Pierre Teilhard de Chardin**

You are an *aspect* of infinite Source consciousness focussed in to a particular point in space and time and as such, you represent a unique component part of pure consciousness. This makes you Divine, perfect and powerful. Like pure Source Energy, you also have creative abilities that stem from the Higher Mind, in exactly the same way that the Universe was created by it, through this field of pure potential. But why does pure consciousness/Source energy need to separate in order to experience itself? HOW does it experience itself in this way? Let's use the simple example of eating an apple. No matter how much you read, think, imagine or educate yourself on an apple, the taste of it, it's flavour, it's texture, it cannot be compared to the actual *experience* of eating it. In the same way, Source energy experiences itself *through* your existence and your creations and your thoughts through your journey through life. The fact that you are alive, have form and the ability to actually think is a testament to your greatness, is proof of your innate connection to Source and the adoration Source has for you. Pure consciousness has <u>thought</u> you into existence, with the intention of fully experiencing a unique aspect of itself whilst equipping you with its spark. When you see yourself as anything less than Divine and deserving of appreciation, or any less perfect than you are, you do yourself and the Creator a huge disservice, placing a limit on your power.

> *'You are not a drop in the ocean, you are the entire ocean in a drop'*
>
> **- Rumi**

As mentioned in the previous chapter, the only reason why we may feel disempowered, the only reason why we would struggle to love ourselves in a divine way is due to an imbalance between our Ego mind and our Heart, in a perceived subconscious attempt to protect ourselves from feeling trauma. The Ego learns very quickly, within the first 5-8 years of life, to trust the words, opinions and teachings of others in order to prevent the pain of further separation, whilst quietening our deeper, inner voice. We learn to trust external opinion over our inner knowing. We learn to act in a way that avoids the feelings of perceived rejection and non-acceptance and come from a place of fear. It is in our initial separation from Source energy that the Ego was actually formed and the more disconnected from Source we feel, the greater the effect of our Ego and therefore our fears.

Just as darkness is not an entity in and of itself but rather the *absence* of light, fear is an absence of cosmic, Source Energy and **LIGHT**, and comes from a perceived lack of connection to it. These symptoms present themselves as a whole host of negative, energetically 'contracting' emotions which affect our wellbeing, health and quality of life. Effectively, the more disconnected we feel from Source, the less energy we have and the more disempowered we feel. The truth is that there is no separation between you and Source, only the illusion of it, solely because of thoughts we habitually think. Negative emotions and movement *away* from wellness are the symptoms of breakdown in our primary relationship – the one we have with our higher being, Source energy. We suffer because we unable to recognise how deeply connected we truly are to it.

The beauty of being in this human form is that we, inherently, have the ability to be on every aspect of the spectrum of consciousness through conscious choice and practice. Picture a hall of mirrors. Effectively we can be in any of the mirrors (versions of reality) through the adjustment of our inner vision. *We* are the Alpha and *we* are the Omega and we have the ability to choose the varying notes of love or lack of love (fear) that reside in between. In order to expand your level of consciousness requires nothing more than the regular observation of your current state and the deliberate intention to change your physical vibration through 'sliding' up the scale of the emotional spectrum. It very much involves practice in residing in your deepest observational state so that you may observe and consciously change your thoughts and emotional states to move more and more towards love. This gradually connects you to infinite consciousness – a platform from which broader perspective, Higher Minded vision, divine inspiration and clarity is readily available. All it takes is for us, in simple words, to **feel good** and the growth takes care of itself.

Chapter 5

Intuition – the third voice

Intuition quite literally means <u>inner teacher</u>. When the five sensory feedback system, historic memory, Ego voice and the interpretation of our external environments is silenced, when the mind is stilled, *space* is created for higher forms of communication.

We can 'tune in' to the background consciousness, in which we all reside and one that permeates everything - the field of **pure potential**. A field of supercharged energy waiting to take form.

Intuition is the underlying 'thinking' and creative aspect of the Universe. By raising our vibration and travelling into deeper states of our being, we return to our core essence and connect with the high vibration of Source energy which communicates via intuition. This energetic cohesion between us and Source closes the gap between the *Alpha* and the *Omega* freeing us from symptoms associated with the illusion of separation. The feelings that we experience as a result of our disconnection, leads to energetic 'misalignment' and fear based symptoms. By changing our state from fear to love helps us to reconnect back to our Source energy. In fact, how we feel is a direct reflection of the strength of our connection to it.

Intuition is the energy that operates within us that is independent of pre-existing thought and feeling. It has no mental dialogue, story and rational basis. Rationality arises from the Mind and the memories of our experience but intuition comes from a Higher Mind. It leads to a surge in pure creative energy and direct communication from Source that channels through us in the absence of energetic resistance and thinking. Intuition is a strong, independent 'gut feeling' that is not based on conscious, mental reasoning. It is an innate knowingness which often leads to a compulsion to act influencing the pre-frontal cortex of the brain.

The intuitive communication from our expanded selves does not occur via regular, mental dialogue or by means our 'monkey mind'. This is because expressions using language are limited due to the potential for varied interpretations just as physical vision is limited, as we discussed in the previous chapters. The way we interpret *all* external stimuli is subject to limitation. For this reason, intuition and higher forms of intelligence do not communicate with us in these ways. Instead they communicate via personal, *internal* methods that are not subject to doubt or misinterpretation. They communicate by means of strong, undeniable visceral feeling, instinct, *inner* vision, a sense of 'knowingness'. Means that go beyond 'regular' forms of communication.

As mentioned previously, whenever we stray from our connection to Source, our Higher Being and our primary relationship, we immediately feel a sense of separation and the feelings associated with it, such as fear, anxiety, helplessness, a lack of control, depression, anger and sadness i.e. lower vibrational states associated with a *lack* of Source energy. When we align with Source however, we feel positive feelings of connection, such as love, excitement, positive anticipation, creativity, inspiration, healing and joy. This is how the 'in built' emotional guidance operates within us. It is designed to assist us in recognizing our alignment with or away from Source which then catalyses our personal expansion and expression. When we align with Source, 'expansive in nature' thoughts, feelings and desires (even of those that are not in our conscious awareness) become supercharged to bloom, and the creative, innovative process begins.

Expansion, as the term suggests, is a natural, resistance-free, form of being. Source energy brings about expansion by means our connection to it, like placing a plug into a socket and switching it on. Nurturing higher vibrational states within us allow this connection to take place and this increases the overall energy within our body, like switching on an electric circuit to allow a current of energy to pass through us. This 'current' floods our energy body and the energy of our deep seated desires (which are like seeds waiting to be watered by Source), building on their energetic momentum and creation. All we have to do is to allow the energy to **FLOW**, by consciously removing 'resistance' which presents itself as denser, negative energy and therefore emotional blocks.

Whenever we take steps to raise our vibration and to *genuinely* feel good, we reap the benefits of our connection to Source. The *'how will creation happen?'* type questions are looked after and we are guided to take the relevant, present moment steps towards our expansion via intuitive communication. Source energy is intelligent, nurturing and encouraging, and sustained connection to it leads to the development of authentic, divine power. Source energy has the broadest perspective of all, a perspective that we do not have full access to.

Subsequently, it can be trusted to know the 'bigger picture' and to guide us in the direction of our bliss.

PERSONAL POWER.

Anything that is considered 'powerful' suggests the absence and removal of resistance and the same applies to our energetic state. In fact, it takes more force and actually *drains* energy to go against expansion and feels like pain of disconnection. Resistance is caused by *contraction* and contraction is caused by negative emotion within our physical field. It presents as lethargy, lack of inspiration and external exertion and manipulation of control – an inauthentic form of power that is used to feel a sense of control within ourselves. These symptoms are very much a consequence of not going with the 'flow' of the Universe, of maintaining resistance (consciously or unconsciously) and going against our connection to Source.

Regardless of external circumstance, we have control over our internal environments. It is sometimes said that 10% of life is what happens to us and 90% of life is how we respond to it.

Through choice we can become empowered in any given circumstance. We have the innate ability to access our authentic power and higher, broader minded perspective just by raising our personal vibration. Just by changing one thought to another and moving up the emotional wellness scale, we have the ability to connect with our expanded selves, to see the 'bigger', broader minded picture and remove limits on our perspective and therefore being. Just as all forms of nature have the ability to thrive in supportive environments, expansion and growth are <u>innate potentials</u> that we are born with. If we cultivate our ability to provide the perfect inner environment for them to thrive, abundance (in all forms) is ours.

We are born *successful* by nature and these expansive, influential states thrive when the resistance within our being is melted. So it is not so much about achieving success through external effort that brings us to our ultimate goal of inner peace, love and joy, it is more about clearing, regularly and diligently, the *internal* mental barriers that are in the way of you and your greatest self. What restricts Source energy from growing through you is your own limited, accumulated thoughts and the subsequent energetic contraction that arises from them. Energetic expansion or contraction is solely based on our ability to choose the thoughts that encourage one or the other. Whilst we are in an 'unconscious' state and whilst we are unaware of the thoughts that circulate in our minds however, the Mind will carry out the selection process automatically on 'auto pilot' based purely on habit. This leads to a life that is influenced but not one that can be the source of influence. This is also known as disempowerment.

When we maintain and consciously *choose* our connection, space is created for intuitive guidance. Our receptivity and awareness become heightened and we are offered the qualities of Source energy - pure creativity, inspiration, passion, wisdom, guidance, problem solving abilities and broader minded perspective. This intuitive communication is received and enhanced by Heart centred wisdom which works in harmony with Divine Intuition. This connection is brought about by awareness of the Ego and training ourselves to become acutely aware of the present moment.

The intuitive, metaphoric mind is a gift and the rational mind is a faithful servant

Recognising intuitive guidance requires practice and a heightened state of awareness and sensitivity. It is necessary to 'de-program' ourselves from unconscious, repetitive cycles of thinking and to learn how to be mentally still and **PRESENT** to be able to create a container for intuition to surface. This creates space and allows us to be able to detect and differentiate the guidance from mental chatter. We have to learn how to become sensitive (instead of shutting it down) to feeling the changes that occur within the body, which is a highly intelligent consciousness tool used by Intuition to express itself. Connection to Intuition connects us to Source energy (a more subtle, ascended energy form than Intuition requiring even *more* sensitivity) and is heavily dependent upon the observation and understanding of the mind and body, in their *natural*, resistance free states. This is a state we experience when we are young children, where there is a "less thinking, more feeling" policy in place. By learning how to get back to a similar place – a place free of energetic 'density' and mental noise – we recognise intuitive guidance more readily. By doing the work to shine the light of our consciousness on our fears and insecurities, we clear the path for higher intelligence to come in by dissolving the Ego based fears/obstacles. Without awareness of our resistance-free state, we have no baseline to measure intuitive feeling against or space for us to connect with it. Furthermore, if our minds are not in the present moment, we are far too mentally busy to even notice.

One of the best ways to tap into your intuition is to learn how to still the mind, to ask a question and to feel a response in the body. An expanded feeling in the body relates to confirmation. Contraction is disapproval from your higher mind that the trajectory of thought in operation shouldn't be followed. The other methods of communication can be deep seated inner knowing, visualisation and hearing from within. Bear in mind that as intuition has no rational (and therefore mental) basis, the responses cannot stem from the mind or any preexisting thoughts that occur in there. The feelings are very much located in the body and are spontaneous with no pre-existing story. They occur separate to the mind and its logical thinking patterns.

Intuitive guidance becomes harder to sense as we transition through life having been taught how to think, feel and act - which effectively 'numbs' us and reduces our sensitivity to fluctuations that occur within the body. We get accustomed to operating in a mechanical way, constantly thinking and being 'in our heads'. Unless we increase our ability to become sensitive enough to detect these fluctuations, we miss regular signals, signs, feelings and communication from Source and our higher, more expanded being. This sensitivity can be cultivated and increased through simple awareness and mindfulness practices and learning how to be mentally present.

Throughout life, *rational* thinking processes are generally prioritised over those that focus on feeling and sensitivity. This form of programming becomes deeply ingrained and is largely responsible for the emotional disconnection that we feel on a personal and on interpersonal levels. It is also responsible for the limitation on our Divine connection and reaching our full potential. The chronic neglect of our emotions and feelings has created widespread imbalance, an epidemic if you will. The importance placed on the head over the feeling body and heart presents itself as worldwide suffering on subtle and also on grand scales, from the energetic and emotional to physical suffering. In fact, the majority of the suffering in the world is a result of this imbalance and our deteriorating connection with infinite consciousness. Everywhere we look, we can see varying symptoms of the same problem – disconnection.

The good news is that we can strip back the layers and unlearn what we have learnt. We can realign, get back on course and reveal our authentic, inner light.

The power of mental presence paired with increased sensitivity to intuitive guidance is a natural state of being and a gift we can reveal and nurture. Moving away from being in the future and past tenses mentally and moving from head to heart allows us to connect with our greatest source of energy, helps us to have faith in the unknown, eliminates fear and ignites our passion. This deep connection to Source is our greatest and our primary relationship.

Remember who you are.
You are made from the Earth and you have come from the stars.

Chapter 6

Finding your Purpose

If it doesn't excite you, it's not the right path

Our purpose surfaces in the presence of passion,
and passion surfaces in the absence of fear.

Where there is passion (and therefore the vibration of genuine gratitude) there is no room for fear, there is no space for the two opposing types of energy to exist together. It defies quantum law. When we feel *genuinely* grateful for something, fear is dispelled and space, a vacuum, is created for excitement and passion to infiltrate. It is virtually impossible to feel any negative emotion when feeling genuine gratitude. Our true purpose starts to reveal itself as our conditioned fears are recognised and cleared through conscious awareness. This process occurs in direct proportion. Our purpose in life is usually very personal and is linked to **THE** <u>core challenge</u> in our lives.

Our work lies in bringing awareness to the multiple influences and the impact of fear in our own lives, including our core wounds and working through them to find our purpose i.e. what it is that we can teach and **EXPRESS** to the world about our transition from fear to empowerment. It is in the sustained commitment to the process of understanding ourselves, understanding what makes us 'tick' and processing fear based beliefs that we align with that which brings us the greatest joy, excitement and passion. It is in the *inward* journey, in the healing of ourselves, that the outward journey is reflected and revealed.

Energetically we draw upon that which mimics our emotional states from the *ether* – the invisible unrefined, raw forms of energy that our senses are generally unable to detect but that which is present all around. The quality of our emotional states and the subsequent attraction of the raw forms of energy can be seen in our environments and circumstances, physically. Just as steam can turn into water and water into ice, our emotional states are the *catalysts* that draw upon the etheric 'steam' which, with sustained focus and momentum, 'crystallise' into physical form. We draw upon and create in exactly the same way that *we* are created, through energetic momentum. When we attach a thought to its corresponding emotion it builds momentum and impacts the etheric field. If this is sustained, the energy will build until the desired outcome is achieved. If, however, we think that we want more wealth but our emotions are focussed on how it feels to <u>not</u> have it i.e. you feel scarcity emotionally, momentum will build toward our emotional state *regardless* of what we think. Our emotions, which are extremely powerful, will impact the etheric field due to the stronger energetic influence they have and override thought.

This process of attraction can occur rapidly or very slowly (even spanning over multiple lifetimes) depending upon our mental focus, the emotional intensity and the momentum that has built as a result. If thought and emotion are aligned, creation happens faster. This may sound simple enough - it makes sense that if we put our minds to a task, it can come into fruition – but the emphasis here is very much the energy of our *emotions* which are quite often underestimated and sometimes neglected collectively. To create on a very small scale, the clarity of our thoughts, the intensity of our emotions and the overall refinement is not as critical although there has to be some alignment or the process cannot occur. To create on a large scale however (to change our lives for the better for example) our thoughts need to be more refined and focussed, our emotions need to be more streamlined and targeted, and the actions (which is the easy part) as a result take care of themselves. Action becomes natural and full of enthusiasm – everything just flows. It cannot be emphasised enough that emotional integrity and emotional energy is *vital* when it comes to the creative process. Without taking these steps, 'fractures' can appear in our energetic projections (and therefore our manifestations) and the creative process will stagnate and lose its sense of playfulness.

Emotions have a major influence on our energy and our aura. The more positive and loving our emotions (which includes love directed at ourselves) the greater the quality of the energy that is projected by our body. There is increased cohesion of our energy field i.e. it becomes more organised, stronger and therefore more expansive. The more expansive our energy, the more influence it has on our surroundings. At our highest emotional states, our ability to connect with the highest frequencies of all increases. This higher frequency of energy is the background, foundational, *deepest possible* 'canvas' of life – Source energy. Being an expanded aspect of ourselves, Source energy acts *alongside* our emotional desires, influencing the ether that surrounds us to bring about our desires generated from a Soul level.

Energy cannot be destroyed, it only changes form and so the energy of our Soul becomes 'imprinted' by the energy of our desires, our fears and our past experiences. These imprints and emotional states of our Soul manifest themselves in our lives at some stage or another. We can direct what is manifested by bringing ourselves, our emotions, our fears, our desires and our entire being into awareness, from which we can select which vibrations to act upon and which to consciously 'clear'.

The process of manifestation not only applies to our active conscious thoughts and their attached emotions but also to our subconscious thoughts, which have the potential to go completely unnoticed. Whilst in an unconscious state, we may unknowingly allow these thoughts to run in the background quite like a software program, whilst they build momentum and intensity. These background vibrations have the potential to attract unfavourable circumstances over time if they are 'low' vibration in nature. The only way we can direct our lives towards favourable circumstances is by becoming more aware of which thoughts are in operation and getting to know ourselves on deeper levels, so that we may become *conscious* directors of our lives rather than unconscious ones.

Our circumstances and external environments act to show ourselves *to* ourselves, not as a means of punishment or reward but by means of Universal law, attraction and magnetism. This is the premise of *karma* – you get back what you give out. Just as warm climates attract birds in winter by use of the electromagnetic grid of the earth, we also create an electromagnetic *pull* on the ether of the Universe via the projection of our thoughts and emotions. In this example, we could say that we are the warmer environment, the birds represent our circumstances and our energetic state creates the magnetic attraction. As it stands in this example, we will attract to ourselves circumstances that *harmonise* with our environment i.e. those that mirror our state.

Every undesirable experience in our lives offers us the opportunity to reflect on those aspects of ourselves that require attention, awareness or readjustment. Picture life to be a constantly running movie and our subconscious/conscious thoughts (as well as our Soul imprints) being the *projectors* creating the scenes of the film. These scenes are dictated by the quality and the nature of the energy we hold and therefore project. Life is the most realistic hologram of our perceptions and when we recognise this, they can be used to assess the projection of our energy. As mentioned previously, there is virtually *no* substance to any structure. What we see around us is a beautiful dance between energy and light and not much else. The projector of our minds *bend* light to create the reality around us. When we clear our limited, lower vibrational, ingrained perceptions, a form of healing takes place. The 'lens' of the projector becomes clearer and we effectively allow our light to 'shine'. We start to become well and whole and this starts to reflect in our lives.

'Thoughts are Universally, not individually, rooted
- Paramhansa Yogananda

Being an integral part of expanded consciousness, the underlying fabric of energy, a Higher Mind, everything that we ever aspire to achieve, or think about, is present all around us in raw, *unrefined* forms of energy. Every 'thing' and every raw 'ingredient' exists around us, in (A) *processed*, physical form and (B) *unrefined*, energetic form. The marriage of the two leads to creation. *All* form that we see around us are the manipulation of energy at a quantum level. If we can imagine something, it already exists in energetic form otherwise it would be impossible to perceive, imagine or be thought. The energetic configuration of thought form has to come from *somewhere* before it is sensed and brought into our awareness. It is not spontaneously created in the mind – energy cannot be created or destroyed, so it has to be energetically present already before our mind considers it.

If you were to fill up a pantry with every single ingredient known to man, you could imagine the most unique recipe using the ingredients and it would be completely possible to achieve. The pantry can be compared to the Universe that contains all of the ingredients and raw materials required for creation to occur. Some 'recipes' may be more difficult to create than others and may also require more refinement, some may not even be a success, but effectively, if you can imagine it, it is possible to find the energetic ingredients to catalyse a product from this abundant, Universal pantry. The same stands true for the manifestation of our desires. Every thought has been drawn down from the ether, where infinite thoughts and their corresponding energies exists.

The Universe is where every single Universal ingredient to manifest is available. This includes what is tangible and what is not – including the energetic configuration of our thoughts, as mentioned above. Everything *beyond* our observational mind i.e. every 'thing' in this Universe, is a tangible form of energy at its core. Our thoughts have substance. The Universe is an infinitely abundant place where our imaginative potential and therefore, our creative potential, is endless. This has been the fundamental understanding of *every* great inventor, creator and manifestor that has existed throughout time.

Although it may be the norm for us now, there was a time when the idea of a 500 ton, aluminum alloy flying through the skies was completely absurd but now the reality of the common airplane is a perfectly accepted aspect of our lives. The creation of the plane came about in the same way – the gradual, conscious building of layers of energy through focus and vision, based on quantum law, until its physical formation.

Effectively, everything we could possibly think of, want or even imagine is all around us in etheric form. In order to fulfil our desires, we can use Universal laws to process them into physical form. Like in the pantry example above, the raw ingredients are available to us but it is in the studying, careful selection, measuring and *alignment* of ingredients, followed by the 'cooking' process that creation occurs. Additionally, the fulfilment of our desires is driven by vision (the recipe), the selective choosing of our thoughts (the ingredients), balancing our emotions (measuring of ingredients) and bringing all component parts together into balance. It is a *flawless* recipe and the only one that has ever been used to create anything. Passion or love create the perfect 'cooking' environments due to their high vibrational and energetic influence on the ether. Fear, effectively, turns the oven *'off'*.

Our true purpose and the fulfilment of our desires however is not exactly the same thing albeit intertwined. Desire can be based on a foundation of fear whereas true purpose is a complete absence of it and operates from a state of passion instead. For instance, we may desire the accumulation of money based on the positive association between money and increased opportunity and the ability to be *more* of who we are. If we desire money based on all the positive aspects associated with it and if we can emotionally *feel* its presence to bring about an energetic change within, a chain reaction is initiated and our desires can be fulfilled. This occurs in a state of passion and happens in the absence of fear. On the flip side, the desire for money can also develop due to an associated fear and the apparent *lack* of it. A constant feeling of not having enough money and its associated fear can lead to a desire by *default* – a desire to break free from pain and fear, perpetuated by further fear. This emotional state is not driven by love and therefore does not direct us toward our passions or our fullest, most balanced lives making it unsustainable and/ or counterproductive.

Passion is independent of our circumstances and our fear based emotions. Our purpose lies in the bringing together of our passions like the pieces of a jigsaw puzzle revealing the bigger picture. Our purpose reveals itself when the energy of Source (the highest vibration) meets the energy of our personality at *its* highest vibration.

Desire based on fear and desire based on unconditional love (passion) is often difficult to differentiate, because:

Fear can *disguise* itself as Love.

Love has the potential to be mistaken for the absence of *discomfort*. This is a limiting, incomplete form of love which is not the pure, authentic love that is necessary for growth or for revealing our purpose to us. Pure love is boundless and unconditional, and is not determined by the presence or absence of any external factors.

If, for example, you develop a fear of travel as a result of being told as a child that the world is a dangerous place to be in, you may grow up being less adventurous and less inclined to explore your surroundings. You may perceive this as a 'love' of being indoors or a 'love' of safe routine. It is, however, love by default. It is influenced by a preconceived belief system about the world in general, based on a foundation of fear. So as comfortable, as safe, as warm and as 'fuzzy' as it may feel to stay indoors all day, to someone who has this belief system, these feelings of 'love' are actually fear in disguise.

In a similar way, we may be lulled into a false sense of love throughout our lives, based upon conditioning and limiting beliefs about ourselves and others. We may be in romantic relationships that are unloving, because we have a fear of being alone, or we may stay in unfulfilling jobs for years because we believe that we are unable to do better. We may confuse love with 'playing it safe' and put a ceiling on our fulfilment, which is effectively a lack of love for *ourselves*.

Fear is comfortable. Love requires courage.

Following on from the above point where it may be clear to see that 'playing it safe' emotionally may not be a true indicator of authentic love, we move on to another difference between love and fear in an attempt to answer the question 'How do we know the difference between Love and Fear in order to find our purpose?'

There is no growth without discomfort. Love encourages growth and fear is restrictive. Growth is the *marker* of love. Love requires the courage to push through discomfort and limitations, and fear forces us into a comfort zone. A comfort zone feels very safe but in order to expand and grow - which I believe is the purpose of life - discomfort and pain shouldn't be 'avoided at all cost'. Expansion and growth are the true indicators of love and the embracing of them should be a life's pursuit. Having the courage to face and move *through* adversity, to allow personal growth, is the ultimate act of *self*-love, and self-love is the foundation of **ALL** forms of the external expression of love. So, remember, just because it is comfortable, it doesn't necessarily mean you are on the path of love and if you are not on the path of love, you are on the path of fear instead. There is no in between.

47

Fear is programmed into us. Love requires self-discovery.

In order to be on the path of love, we go against thousands of years of conditioned thinking patterns. This means that sometimes it is easier, and even *encouraged*, to give in to fear. Throughout generations and our upbringing, whether it be consciously or not, we have been taught to be fearful of a whole host of things, from actual danger to beliefs about how we look or dress and even how we should and shouldn't think. By being programmed to think and feel in a particular way, we lose our ability to do *either* and this is not a quality of authentic love. Authentic love does not disable us or others. Love feels like freedom.

Love requires emotional intelligence and self-awareness which is not readily taught by society or even our well-wishing parents. This fear/love imbalance in our *internal* environments is responsible for a whole host of emotional and mental imbalances that we see in society today. Fear, insecurity and a lack of self-worth can become advantageous, not just monetarily to large institutions but falsely even to *ourselves*, as we become convinced that we are benefitting by thinking in a fearful way. We can get lulled us into a false sense of safety and security. Whenever we think thoughts such as 'I can't do this, so I won't try' or 'I'm not good enough' we are suffering from symptoms of this conditioning and imbalance - an imbalance that we were not born with but one that we have learned and made into a habit.

So how do we break the cycles of fear based thinking?

By becoming more <u>conscious</u> of our own fears; by bringing our 'darkness' into the 'light'; by merging the *Yin* and the *Yang* aspects; by knowing ourselves and by becoming aware of who we are and how we think. We break the cycles of fear by choosing the course of our thoughts and therefore our lives. By choosing the path of Love or the path of Fear.

Through self-awareness and connection to our bodies, we can free ourselves from the bondage of fear, live a peaceful, loving and joyful life, connect to divinity and become a source of inspiration for others.

Love is power. Fear is force.

Being in a loving state should empower and **EXCITE** you.

It should make you feel energised since love *expands* energy. Fear backs you into a corner and restricts you with an opposing force. Love is therefore powerful, expansive and activates passion. In any given situation, choosing love i.e. the absence of fear on a strong foundation of self-love directs you towards your passions and your fulfilment. Choosing this state over and over again, and being in this sustained state will guide you towards the recognition of your purpose. It aligns you with external forms of love and abundance. This form of mental alchemy, turning lead into gold, aligns you with your natural state of being, your true essence and tunes you into a powerful source of loving/expansive energy that guides and directs you towards your Souls purpose and desires.

'Opportunity is missed by most people because it is dressed in overalls and looks like work'

- Thomas A. Edison

When we have discovered our purpose, when we are aware of what we want, when we discover those ideas that get us out of bed in the morning with joyous enthusiasm, the next step is to ***ground*** our passions into physical form. This is the second phase of manifestation – the external, material manifestation. Just thinking and emotions alone (the internal aspects) will not bring about enough momentum for your physical reality to manifest itself. The great thing about grounding, is that it's the easiest part. When thoughts and emotions are aligned, physical creation happens with ease due to the amount of energy that is behind it. It becomes more difficult, in fact, to take *no* action. We have done this our entire lives, yet in order to have the life we desire, we need to become conscious creators rather than unconscious ones so that we may direct our lives towards our passions rather than towards our fears.

Creation occurs at three levels – the thought, the word and the deed. Our thoughts need to be aligned with our words and our words need to be aligned with our actions. In order to manifest successfully (whether it be consciously for our growth or unconsciously for our contraction), all three need to operate in harmony and with integrity – they must mirror and reflect each other.

For example:

You're thirsty. You want to make a cup of tea.

First comes the awareness that you are thirsty, then comes the internal dialogue followed by the choice of thought resulting in 'I will make myself a cup of tea', then comes the act of making it.

All manifestations follow these principles:

Awareness,

Inner dialogue,

Choice,

Result.

In the above example, from the awareness of thirst comes the *thought*. From the thought comes the *word* or the internal dialogue and then comes the *deed* or the action of making yourself a drink. Awareness and action are relatively automatic but the thought and internal dialogue is where our greatest influence lies – in that space in between thoughts. It is mastering energy at this level that we create the inner alchemy and the maximum impact on our lives.

The recognition of subconscious and conscious thinking patterns assist in the awareness of our inner, present moment mental dialogue from which place thoughts and circumstances that benefit us can be *consciously* selected and emphasised and those that do not can be *consciously* given less focus.

The *emphasised* thoughts then become our emotional, and therefore energetic state - the vibrations of which we emit into the Universe and ultimately attract back to us electromagnetically.

The idea is to allow **ALL** thoughts entry into our mind space to begin with and not to control any of them, so that they can be seen. From the wonderful array of thoughts and perceptions, we can choose our mental direction based on the information that make us feel the greatest levels of love and excitement i.e. we can choose to operate from a higher vibrational state just by choosing thoughts that make us feel the best. Aligning our thoughts, with our words and our deeds 'clears the path' for Universal energies to infiltrate our being as we align with it (the famous **NAMASTE** hands) which then acts as a source of inspiration, guidance, support and the driving force behind the fulfilment of our desires. This is influence and connection at the deepest level.

'If you are depressed you are living in the past.
If you are anxious you are living in the future.
If you are at peace you are living in the present.'
- Lao Tsu

Thoughts stemming from the past and based on the future are a huge reason why we experience emotions associated with fear based thinking – a habit of thinking that we have all developed during our lives at some point or another. When we use our minds to access the past and future tenses as and when required, rather than residing there, we learn about the huge benefits of presence. The present moment is where we can feel wellness and peace; where our minds are still and where we have greatest influence. It is also the place where we are able to 'listen' to inner and Universal wisdom. Presence is where we can move *out* of our busy minds and connect with our bodies, which prompt us to our vibrational states and put us back in touch with our personal power. The past is memory, the future is imagination and so in many cultures they are considered the illusions of time.

Finding your purpose is a process that can take days, years, decades and even lifetimes. This process, however, can be accelerated through a number of practices to 'weed out' fear and raise our vibration – techniques that are from both modern day practises and going back *thousands* of years. They are tools that expand our awareness, raise our vibration and can support us if we have the will and commitment to know ourselves and clear subconscious, restrictive thinking patterns. Such tools include contemplation, meditation, mindfulness, breathing techniques, energy healing, yoga, chi kung, floatation, sound vibration, binaural beats and so many more. Even a simple practice of routine can help us to reach these more enlightened states. These practices are designed to bring us back to our centre, bring our minds back to the present moment, connect us to ourselves on deeper levels and to tune us back in to our true power.

Chapter 7

What is Alignment?

Energetic alignment is a fusion between defragmented aspects of our being.

It exists at two levels:
1. At the *physical* level: the alignment between what we think, what we say and what we do.
2. At the *non-physical* level: the alignment between our conscious mind, our subconscious mind and the superconscious mind.

Wholeness comes from the merging of the physical with the non-physical. Alignment is the single greatest catalyst for wellbeing, abundance, connection, peace of mind, overall success and fulfilment of desire. When aligned, we connect *deeply* with our inner being, our broader minded perspective and Source energy. We become absolute *powerhouses* for change. In our lives and in the lives of others.

PHYSICAL alignment.

Physical alignment occurs when what we *think*, what we *say* and what we *do* are in harmony. When these three factors are out of alignment, fragmentation of our energy occurs. This leads to the creation of a somewhat 'disconnected' vibration which is emitted from the body into the aura and into the ether, impacting all three energetically. This discorded energy is 'sent out' which, with enough momentum, attracts experiences of a similar nature – discorded - whether it be discord within our bodies or discord in our circumstances.

For instance, if you are in the pursuit of accumulating money, your actions may be aligned with this desire and so may your words but if you *think* that money is difficult to obtain or if you associate money with difficult emotional experiences, your resultant energetic vibration will be fragmented.

Similarly, if you are in the pursuit of love, you may have underlying beliefs about love that are limiting, based on painful historic experience. Unless your sense of awareness is raised enough to be able to observe and clear these limiting beliefs, your actions, words and thoughts will work against each other to create energetic resistance, defragmentation and you won't be able to reach (or at the least, keep) your goal.

We are, innately, extremely powerful creators. We constantly create the circumstances and experiences around us. The only factor that prevents us from creating *desirable* circumstances for ourselves, is the amount of energetic resistance we build throughout our lives. What this suggests is that all the good things in life are ready to flow to us and we are holding them back through our own resistance. We are connected to the background, abundant, flawlessly creative, energy field and we therefore ARE it. Abundance is our nature. This connection gives us life and fulfils our desires and it is in the resistance to this connection that prevents us from channeling our creative abilities.

The process of creation begins at the level of thought. What we say (internal and external dialogue) and what we *do* are the resultant effects of the momentum that is built by our thoughts. The alignment of all three, the Holy Trinity, is a powerful force that leads to the manifestation of desires. It is therefore important for us to become regularly aware of our thoughts, until we become a state of presence, in order to *fuel* the manifestation of consciously selected, desirable outcomes. Our emotions and their associated physical sensations, are of extreme value when it comes to raising our awareness and recognising which thoughtsare in operation. In fact, all emotions can be directly traced back to an individual or a closely related group of thoughts. By themselves, thoughts can be difficult to identify but with the help of the body, we can see and understand our mental dialogue with greater ease. For example, thoughts which relate to grief cause contraction in the chest. Thoughts associated with shame can cause contraction in the pelvic area of the body. As mentioned previously, for us to recognise the regular signals that our bodies are giving to us, we must increase our overall sensitivity to the minor and major changes that occur within them. This sensitivity allows us to recognise deviations *away* from resistance-free, centred states.

Alignment cannot occur without 'unearthing' resistant conscious and subconscious thoughts and their associated feelings. This is because without their awareness, even if they are not present in the conscious mind, they can impact our physical vibration and manifestations. The good news is that since our external environments i.e. our thoughts, our emotions, our physical states and our circumstances are reflections of our internal states, life is consistently reflecting our vibration back to us. The trick is to be able to identify these 'lessons' and to use them as platforms to grow. The awareness of resistant thoughts is a form of energetic 'clearing'. We shine the light of our consciousness onto our inner blind spots. The process becomes more efficient over time, with practice in heightening our sensitivity levels and in regularly residing in the present moment. In our observer mind.

Some of our vibratory 'imprints' can also come from past lives, since the nature of energy is that it cannot be destroyed and can only change form. These imprints on the Souls' energy can either catalyse expansion or contraction i.e. they can be love or fear based too. They can be transported into our physical existence and be in operation in our current lives.

All of the resistant energy that needs to be cleared from our being become easier to identify as we go 'up' the sensitivity scale.

<u>NON PHYSICAL</u> alignment.

This level of alignment occurs when the *subconscious, conscious and superconscious* minds operate in harmony with each other. These are the three levels of consciousness that are in operation at any given time. They are the layers of our mind.

The <u>conscious</u> mind is the platform that we operate from during our daily activities and during waking hours. It represents only a small portion of our consciousness and is the aspect of our mental processing that we can think and talk about in a rational way. It is the logical aspect of our minds. The conscious mind involves all of the things that you are currently aware of and thinking about. Things that the conscious mind wants to keep hidden from our awareness, such as painful memories, are repressed into the *subconscious* mind where they do not always have a strong logical reason to be there. These subconscious thoughts can be drawn upon through conscious awareness and via various methods and 'triggers'. The conscious mind is somewhat akin to short term memory and is limited in terms of its capacity.

The <u>subconscious mind</u> accounts for approximately 80% of our consciousness and lies *below* the level of conscious awareness. Its physical seat in the body is in the lower brain and the spine. It records *everything* that we do or have done, including every activity we have ever engaged in, our thoughts about those activities and their associated emotions. For the most part, this aspect of our consciousness remains hidden from our everyday awareness and often 'leaks' into our conscious minds in disguised form. An example of this is when historic memory is triggered by even a *loosely* linked external event, leading to an extremely realistic mental overlay on our present circumstances.

The subconscious mind has tremendous influence on how we think and act when in a conscious state. Those influences are from <u>past actions</u> and the subsequent habits and perceptions that we have formed from them. What this means is that ideas that are drawn from the subconscious mind are not *new* or *creative* in nature and so operating from this aspect of our minds is limiting and repetitive. When the subconscious mind is understood and cleared of denser energies and thoughts, it provides a channel for the communication between the conscious and the *superconscious* mind.

The superconscious mind encompasses a level of awareness that sees both material reality and also the *energy* behind that reality. It has a wider perspective of reality. Through observation, clearing and the raising of our personal vibration, we melt resistance which allows us to tune into superconsciousness.

Superconsciousness is also known as Source energy, God, the Universe, the Field and a variety of other references. Essentially, it is the deepest layer of our being. The superconscious is not tangled by historic experience and so is where *true* creativity is found. As a result of our connection to it, we draw upon the creative potential that has created all that is. Expressions of this kind of creativity are distinctive from those that come from the conscious or the subconscious mind – they are new, innovative and expansive. Not just expanding the mind but also our being. Truly great works of art, music, the greatest scientific discoveries and the deepest spiritual experiences stem from the superconscious mind.

"We have to remember that what we observe is not nature herself, but nature exposed to our method of questioning"

– Werner Heisenberg – founder of Quantum Mechanics

When we raise our energetic vibration and consciousness to access the superconscious mind, we have the ability to access the thoughts that are available on *that* level of consciousness. These thoughts are universally available to those who tune in at this level. Similarly, if we live mainly on conscious or subconscious levels, we operate using thoughts from those respective levels which then become reflected in our reality. Due to its nature, operating from a purely conscious mind, we see *distinction* between us and others - but operating from a superconscious level we are less limited in our perspectives and are able to see the underlying unity – the energetic reality – behind outer form. This is a form of psychic attunement to higher intelligence.

The merging and <u>unity</u> of all of the aspects of our being – our thoughts, feelings, emotions, dialogue, actions, subconscious, superconscious and conscious mind is heavily dependent on and *directly* related to the **awareness** of all aspects. With awareness comes expansion, spontaneous clearing, wellness, wholeness, connection and creativity. You enter into a state called Love.

Alignment opens us up to higher forms of intelligence, a deep sense of wisdom, inner knowing and pure vision. We see the perfection of all of life. We shift from the smaller, personality mind to our expanded, Divine, **HIGHER** mind and are able to live out our authentic essence, purpose and passions.

Chapter 8

❦

Fill up your cup

Alignment and our connection to Source energy is heavily dependent on the *state* that we operate in. Our physical state is a reflection of our emotional state. The more empowered our state, i.e. the more expansive it is, the higher the vibration of our energetic output and the more connected we are.

A powerful, healthy, 'high' vibrational state occurs in the presence of good feeling emotion, such as happiness, joy, exuberance, love and hope. High vibrational states are reflected in our physical bodies too and we feel more energetic and motivated. A 'lower' vibrational state leads to feelings such as depression, sadness, loneliness, anger, despair, anxiety and hopelessness. This, too, is reflected in our bodies as an overall <u>reduction</u> in energy. Effectively, lower vibrational, fear-based emotions create an internal state that increases resistance and prevents growth. It also prevents cosmic, Source energy from flowing into our energy body which in turn affects our alignment with it, makes us feel drained and makes us feel like we are running on empty.

Our physical and emotional states are a reflection of our thoughts. The conscious, deliberate selection of 'good feeling' thoughts has a direct impact on our emotions and therefore our body.

Similarly, changes in our body have a direct impact on our thoughts and emotions too. The mind, body and spirit are all interlinked and connected. Energy flows between them. Understanding our state, at any given time, by becoming aware of our thoughts, emotions and how our body feels can put us in a place of power, where we can alter our vibrational output through choice. We are the only beings on earth that have this ability.

Initially it is much easier to gain information on the quality of our states by connecting with and detecting changes in the body first, as the momentum of energy is greater in our body than when they were created in our thoughts. Over time and with practice, as our sensitivity increases, we are able to detect changes in our mental balance i.e. at the point of creation. We can more easily detect deviation away from our centre point which is firmly in the present moment.

<u>All you have to do is take the first step</u>

On a strong foundation of self-love, self-care and attention directed towards ourselves, we are able to 'love' ourselves into higher states. By becoming aware of that which brings us discomfort, by honouring our emotions enough to pay attention to them and by <u>soothing</u> the associated thoughts into thoughts of a loving nature, we reverse momentum and change the frequency at which we vibrate.

At times this may involve removing yourself physically from a particular situation that causes vibrational imbalance at other times it may involve choosing thoughts that feel better by being the 'calm in the storm'. These boundaries need to placed by ourselves based on what feels the best. Emotions such as gratitude and appreciation are powerful states to be in, strong enough to create a state in which lower vibrational thoughts, stemming from fear, cannot exist. As mentioned previously, it is almost *impossible* to feel negative emotion when we feel genuine gratitude. Training our brains to reside in these states is of huge value when it comes to creating desirable outcomes. This practice takes us back to our authentic nature. Starting the day with feelings of gratitude or even a 'thank you' creates energetic momentum in the direction of our desires. It leads to expansion of our state and strengthens our connection to ourselves and to Source.

By starting the process of manifestation i.e. finding and selecting single positive aspects to focus on that feels good - energetic momentum starts to build. Thoughts of a similar nature get drawn upon to create further momentum. Your energy body expands and you vibrate 'higher'. Over time, alignment takes place and you connect with the all-encompassing field. From this place, *more* energy is drawn down from expanded, abundant Source which aligns with you. You experience deep connection.

This connection then presents to you circumstances, situations and people that help you to close the gap between you and your Souls' purpose and inner fulfilment. Following Heart centred wisdom by means your intuition, you can use *feeling* to keep moving back into *alignment* and then *action* which createsfurther expansion and desirable circumstances. This creates even *greater* levels of energy, momentum and connection. Once the mind has expanded, it can never go back. It keeps on expanding.

This is a journey from head to heart. An energetically flawless, *tried and tested* formula. All you have to do is from this present moment, take the first step.

Protecting your energy.

As your energetic sensitivity increases, it is not only possible to tune into changes that occur within your personal energy field, it is also possible that you will tune into the energy fields of others.

Just as important it is to be able to discern higher vibrational thoughts from lower vibrational ones within ourselves, it is equally as important to discern which energies exist within you that are *yours* and which energies belong to others. Some people can walk into a room and light up the entire room, others can drag the vibration down based on their level of consciousness. Often we can take on the energies of those around us, adopting them as our own. As a result, we can create momentum based on *their* energies. It is therefore crucial to clear your energy and your energetic 'vessel' regularly to clear lower vibrational energies and to be able to continue expansion. Bear in mind that if we are too conscious of "protecting" ourselves from others it comes from a place of fear, this can go against the purpose of alignment. There is a difference between discerning which direction to move in and shielding ourselves.

Unconditional love is the goal as it is the *highest* frequency that we can resonate at. This level of unconditional love must spread to ourselves too in order for us to be whole and for us to operate from a place of vibrational integrity. This means being kind to ourselves when things don't feel right and placing healthy boundaries. Practising energetic detachment from our thoughts and from others and by operating from a place of deep observation creates space for unconditional love to blossom. The result is that we *emit* loving energy rather than absorbing denser energy. This is not only an act of unconditional love aimed at ourselves but also directed at others and <u>true</u> influence. Energetic detachment moves us away from dependency and is the path towards higher forms of love.

Being in an 'observer' state and detaching from our thoughts and emotions to be able to see them, takes time and practice. The first stage is to acknowledge changes in our states and to *accept* them for what they are – self-love. The second stage is to observe them from a distance and to create space to do this. Sometimes the extent of detachment needs to be greater i.e. physically removing yourself from a situation and at other times it requires nothing more than mentally creating space by changing our minds. Whichever method is adopted is it important to understand that there is no 'right' or 'wrong' way.

Our evolution towards unconditional love and the freedom of detachment from our thoughts occurs in the understanding and the awareness of who we are. It is for this reason that the greatest philosophers and teachers of our time have placed massive emphasis on 'knowing thyself'. This simple yet profound statement encompasses the entire content of this book. It summarizes the key to our success in two simple and genius words, the brief explanation of which has been the aim for this piece of writing.

I hope that this aim has been achieved. If nothing else, I hope this book has opened your mind to some degree and inspired you to carry on your search for greatness.

Seek and ye shall find.

Dare to have vision and break free of your conditioning. Dare to be free.

My wish is that fear never holds you back. What you desire is attainable. If you can imagine it, the energy of it already exists in the ether. Understand and train your mind – you have infinite opportunities. A successful mindset attracts success in life.

'While the world of reality has its limits, the world of your imagination is without boundaries. Learn to recognise the signs of habitual ways of being and then learn to shift your thinking to being in balance with your dreams'

- Dr. Wayne Dyer

Chapter 9

Future Events

Join me and my Soul family at the
'Get Conscious' Magic, Mystery and Self Mastery Retreats

where you can learn how to connect with your
Body, Mind, Intuition and your
Higher Minded perspective.

Visit
www.getconscious.co.uk

for up to date information and 121 services

Follow us on Facebook and Instagram at *'Get Conscious'*

Email us for individual and corporate bookings at:
hello@getconscious.co.uk

*'Until you make the unconscious conscious, it
will direct your life and you will call it fate.'*
- Carl Jung

Printed in the United States
By Bookmasters